SNACKtivities

No-bake treats
Kids can make

Bible story activities for ages 2 to 5

by Karyn Henley

Karyn Henley's SNACKtivities

Bible story activities for children ages 2 to 5

Written and illustrated by Karyn Henley
Editing and Layout by Kristi J. West

Dandelion logo is a registered trademark of Karyn Henley

For more information about this curriculum, contact:

Karyn Henley Resources
PO Box 40269
Nashville, TN 37204-0269

1-888-573-3953 (toll-free U.S.)

www.karynhenley.com

A word about **photocopying**:

Printed in the U.S.A

Table of Contents

Table of Contents

SNACKtivities

No-Bake Treats Kids Can Make

Fruity Cream Cheese Sandwich

Ingredients
soft cream cheese
fresh seedless red and green grapes
thin-sliced wheat bread

Kitchen Tools
knife for teacher's use
mixing bowl, spoon
paper plates, plastic knives
paper towels

Prepare Ahead of Time
Wash the grapes and cut in half.

Guide Each Child To
1. Help put the cream cheese into a bowl.
2. Add grapes and stir mixture.
3. Dip some of the mixture onto a piece of bread and spread it with a plastic knife.
4. Place another slice of bread on top.
5. Put the sandwich on a paper plate and eat it.

Variation: Substitute toasted English muffins halves for the bread. Stir 1/2 cup of preserves (any flavor) into 8-ounces of cream cheese. Spread on English muffin halves. Have the children help prepare this snack and use with the "Thank-You" Bible stories listed below.

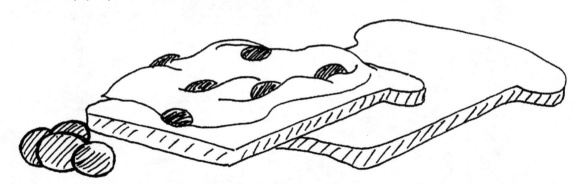

Suggested Bible Stories
Grapes:
Twelve Spies
Two Sons and a Vineyard

Thank-You:
David Thanks God
Singers Lead Jehoshaphat's
    Army
Daniel Thanks God
Ten Lepers

Talk About
Grapes:
• What do grapes grow on? What do they look like when they are hanging on the vine? (You may want to show a bunch of grapes.)
• What do grapes taste like? Did you ever taste grape jelly, grape Popsicles, or grape juice?
• Somebody grew grapes or found grapes in our story. Tell about what happened.
Thank-You:
• How did you help to make our snack? Who helped you?
• Why do we tell each other thank-you?
• Who said thank-you in our story? Why?

Rainbow Cake

Ingredients
pound cake or white sheet cake, unfrosted
one 12-ounce tub of whipped topping
1 pint of strawberries, cut into halves
1 pint of blueberries
about 12 peach slices, cut into chunks
2 kiwi fruit, cut into chunks

Kitchen Tools
paper plates, paper towels
plastic knives, forks

Guide Each Child To
1. Help frost the cake with the whipped topping.
2. Help arrange the different colors of fruit across the cake in an arch to form a rainbow. Put blueberries across the top in the first row, kiwi fruit in the second row, peaches in the next row, and strawberries in the last row.
3. Help cut a piece of cake for herself and put it on her plate.

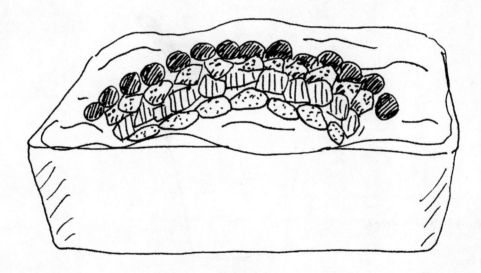

Suggested Bible Stories
Noah
Joseph's Colorful Coat
Jonah
Jesus Stills the Storm
John Sees Heaven (rainbow around the throne, Revelation 4)

Talk About
• Did you ever see a rainbow in the sky? What was it like?
• When do rainbows come into the sky?
• What color do you like best?
• What was colorful in our story? What happened?

Hot Chocolate Mix

Ingredients
8-quart box of powdered milk
2 cups of powdered coffee creamer
8 ounces of instant chocolate drink powder
1/2 cup of powdered sugar
very warm water, not hot

Kitchen Tools
large bowl
mixing spoon
measuring cups
Styrofoam hot cups
plastic spoons

Prepare Ahead of Time
Heat water and store in thermos to keep warm.

<table>
<tr><td>Caution
Carefully supervise
the children when
using hot water</td></tr>
</table>

Guide Each Child To

1. Help measure and mix the powdered milk, coffee creamer, chocolate powder, and powdered sugar in a bowl.
2. Dip 1/3 cup of mix into a Styrofoam cup.
3. Carefully add very warm (not hot) water to make the cup two-thirds full.
4. Stir and drink.

Suggested Bible Stories
Noah
Isaac Is Born
Isaac Gets a Wife
Bitter Water Turns Sweet
Ruth
Singers Lead Jehoshaphat's Army
David Thanks God
Daniel Thanks God
Water Into Wine
The Good Samaritan
The Runaway Son
Ten Lepers
Zacchaeus
The Crucifixion

<table>
<tr><td>Talk About
• Let's thank God before we drink our hot chocolate.
• What's your favorite thing to drink?
• What's your favorite thing to eat?
• Why do we thank God for our food and drink?
• Who was thankful in our story? What were they thankful for?</td></tr>
</table>

Chicken Noodle Soup

Ingredients
canned chicken noodle soup
oyster crackers or fish-shaped crackers

Kitchen Tools
small bowls, spoons
ladle or serving spoon
bowl for crackers

Prepare Ahead of Time
Purchase enough for each child to have a small serving. Heat the soup and store in a thermos to keep warm. Place crackers in a container which will be easy for children to handle.

Guide Each Child To
1. Take a bowl and spoon.
2. Wait for teacher to pour soup into his bowl.
3. Wait a few minutes to allow the soup to cool a bit.
4. Take a few crackers from the cracker container and pass it to another classmate.
5. Eat his soup and crackers.

Caution
Carefully supervise the children when eating hot soup

Suggested Bible Stories
Sharing:
Abraham and the Three Visitors
Birthright and Blessing
Ruth
David and Jonathan
David and Mephibosheth
Elisha's Room on the Roof
Jesus Feeds 5,000
Jesus Makes Breakfast for His Friends
Lydia
Sickness:
Naaman
Through the Roof
The Lame Man at the Pool
The Centurion's Sick Servant
Woman Touches Jesus' Hem
Ten Lepers
Jesus Heals the Bent Woman
The Man's Withered Hand
Peter and John Heal a Lame Man

Talk About
Sharing:
• We're sharing our soup and crackers. What else can you share?
• How do you feel when someone shares with you?
• Who shared in our story?
• Why does God want us to share?
Sickness:
• Sometimes when people get sick, they eat soup, especially chicken soup.
• What do you like to eat when you're sick?
• Who was sick in our story? How did they get well?

English Muffin Animals

Ingredients
2 English muffin halves for each child
soft margarine
raisins

Kitchen Tools
toaster
plastic knives
paper plates

Guide Each Child To
1. Toast two English muffin halves and put margarine on them.
2. Place the English muffin halves on a paper plate.
3. Cut one of the muffin halves in half to make two semicircles.
4. Arrange the muffin halves to be a dog, rabbit, or fish as shown.
5. Place raisins on the animal shapes to make eyes, nose, and mouth.

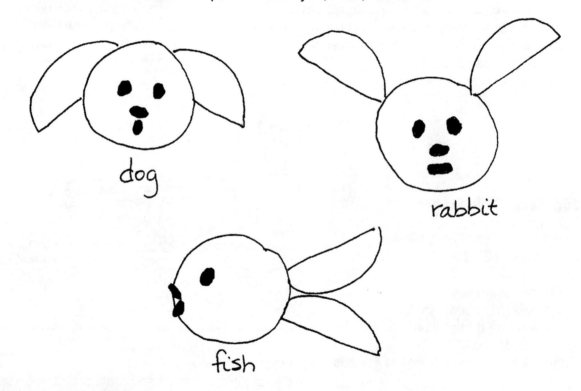

dog

rabbit

fish

Suggested Bible Stories
Creation of Animals
Noah
Rebekah Gives Water to the Camels
Balaam's Talking donkey
Saul Looks for Lost Donkeys
Jonah
The Great Catch of Fish
Tax Money in a Fish
Jesus Makes Breakfast for His Friends

Talk About
• What kind of animal do you like best?
• Do you have an animal at your house?
• How do you take care of your animal?
• What kind of animal was in our story? What happened?

Treasure Salad

Ingredients
4 packages of gelatin (one each of red, yellow, green and blue)

Kitchen Tools
plastic knives, spoons
pancake turner
bowls

Prepare Ahead of Time
Make four bowls of gelatin, one of each color. Use wide bowls or pans so that the gelatin will be about 1-inch deep.

Guide Each Child To
1. Help cut the gelatin, making lines to form 1-inch cubes.
2. Help scoop the gelatin out of each pan onto a plate using a pancake turner. Put one color of gelatin cubes on each plate.
3. Get a bowl and spoon and scoop two of each color of gelatin cube into his bowl.

Suggested Bible Stories
Isaac Gets a Wife
Queen of Sheba
Solomon Builds the Temple
Esther
Hidden Treasure
Bigger Barns

Talk About
• What's a treasure? What are jewels?
• Did you ever see sparkly jewels or fancy jewelry? Where? What was it like?
• What were the treasures, riches, or jewels in our story?

Apple Honey Nutters

Ingredients
1/2 cup of peanut butter
1/4 cup of wheat germ
1/4 cup nonfat dry milk
2 Tablespoons honey
1 apple for every two children

Kitchen Tools
knife for teacher's use
mixing bowl, spoon
measuring spoons, cups
plastic spoons
paper plates, towels

Guide Each Child To
1. Help measure and mix the peanut butter, wheat germ, dry milk, and honey.
2. Watch the teacher cut the apples in half and scoop out the core.
3. Fill the center of the apple with the peanut butter mixture and spread it over the apple.
4. Place the apple on a paper plate and eat the apple honey nutter.

Suggested Bible Stories
Adam and Eve Have a Family
Rebekah Gives Water to the Camels
Joseph in Prison
Baby Moses (Miriam watches and helps)
Ruth
The Good Samaritan
Mary and Martha
Jesus Makes Breakfast for His Friends
Dorcas

Talk About
• How did you help to make these apple snacks?
• Why do we need to help each other?
• How do you help at home? How do you help in class?
• Who was a helper in our story? What happened?

Moon Cookies

Ingredients
pre-made sugar cookies (or another type of cookie with a plain top)
3 cups powdered sugar
1/8 teaspoon salt
1/4 teaspoon orange extract
3 1/2 to 4 Tablespoons orange juice

Kitchen Tools
mixing bowl, spoon
sifter
paper towels
plastic spoons
paper plates

Guide Each Child To
1. Help sift the powdered sugar into the bowl.
2. Add the salt, orange extract, and orange juice to the sugar.
3. Help stir the mixture well.
4. Use a spoon to drizzle the glaze mixture over his cookie.

Suggested Bible Stories
Creation of Sun, Moon, and Stars
Jacob's Dream
Joseph's Dreams
The Sun Stands Still
Gideon
Nicodemus Visits Jesus at Night

Talk About
• When do you see the moon? Did you ever see the moon in the daytime?
• What other lights are in the sky?
• Is the moon always big and round? What shapes can it be?
• Who made the moon?
• It was nighttime in our story. What happened that night?

Cheese Logs

Ingredients (for 14 logs)
one 8-ounce box of cream cheese, well-chilled
12 saltine crackers
one 2-ounce jar of bacon bits

Kitchen Tools
one plastic sandwich bag
knife for teacher's use
mixing bowl, spoon
paper plates, towels

Guide Each Child To
1. Help the teacher slice the brick of cream cheese lengthwise into seven slices. Cut each of the seven slices in half.
2. Put the crackers into the sandwich bag and take turns crushing them.
3. Mix the cracker crumbs and bacon bits in a bowl.
4. Cover the bottom of a paper plate with the crumb mixture.
5. Roll a "log" of cream cheese in the crumb mixture. (As it is rolled in the crumbs it becomes easier to handle and lengthens into a longer roll like a small log.)
6. Put his log onto a paper plate and eat it.

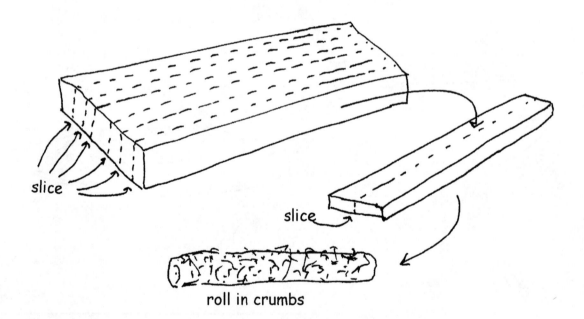

slice

slice

roll in crumbs

Suggested Bible Stories
Noah
Tower of Babel
Solomon Builds the Temple
Elisha's Room on the Roof
Rebuilding Jerusalem's Walls
The Wise Man's House

Talk About
• What's a log? What is it used for?
• How does a house get built?
• What did the people build in our story? What happened?

Happy Face Cookies

Ingredients
pre-made sugar cookies (or another type of cookie with a plain top)
ready to spread frosting in a can or tube
cocktail peanuts*

Kitchen Tools
paper plates
plastic knife

*For children with allergies to peanuts, substitute raisins or candy.
IDEA: Substitute bread or sliced biscuits for the cookies. Use jelly in a squirt bottle to make a happy face.

Guide Each Child To
1. Put a cookie on his plate.
2. Use a little dab of frosting to help "glue" the peanuts onto her cookie to form two eyes and a smile.

Variation: To emphasize *Giving* or *Sharing*, have the children decorate two cookies, one for them and one for a friend. After decorating the cookie, place it in a plastic sandwich bag. Tie the bag with a ribbon to make as a gift to take to someone.

Suggested Bible Stories
Joy:
Isaac Is Born
Jacob and Esau
Hannah Prays for a Baby
Gabriel Appears to Mary
The Triumphal Entry
The Resurrection
The Lost Sheep
The Lost Coin
The Runaway Son
Giving/Sharing:
Joseph's Colorful Coat
Samuel's New Coats
David and Jonathan
Queen of Sheba
A Widow Shares With Elijah
Elisha's Room on the Roof
The Wise Men
Perfume on Jesus' Feet
The Widow's Mite

Talk About
Joy:
• What makes you joyful? Does it make you joyful to help others?
• When someone loves you, does it give you joy? Who loves you?
• How can you tell someone feels joyful?
• Who was joyful in our story? Why? What happened?
Giving/Sharing:
• Who will you give your gift of cookies to?
• Who gave in our story? What did they give? What happened?
• Why does God want us to be cheerful givers?

Barley Soup

Ingredients
canned beef consommé or beef broth
water
barley

Kitchen Tools
Styrofoam cups
plastic spoons
paper towels

Prepare Ahead of Time
Pour the soup into the pan and add one can of water to the soup. Add 1/3 cup of barley to the soup and bring to a boil. Allow soup to simmer on low head for 30 minutes. Put in a thermos to keep soup warm. Bring the soup and some of the uncooked barley in a plastic zip bag or clear container to class.

Caution
Carefully supervise the children when eating hot soup

Guide Each Child To
1. Look at and feel the uncooked barley.
2. Let the teacher pour a small amount of barley soup in his cup.
3. Listen quietly as the teacher talks about barley (see Talk About section below).
4. Make sure soup is not too hot, then and taste it.

Suggested Bible Stories
Joseph's Dreams
Pharaoh's Dreams
Joseph's Brothers Go to Egypt
Ruth
Bigger Barns
The Wheat and the Weeds

Talk About
- The barley is a grain grown in fields. After adding broth, the barley becomes a soup.
- What does the barley look like? Have you ever seen barley before? How does it feel? Does it smell like anything before it is cooked?
- How does the soup smell?
- What other kinds of soup have you eaten before?
- Who gives us our food?

Giant Cookie

Ingredients

pre-made giant cookie from bakery (purchase the large cookie pre-decorated or request a plain cookie and let children decorate it using ready to spread frosting, candy, and sprinkles)

Kitchen Tools

knife for teacher
plastic knife or spoon
small paper plates

Guide Each Child To   (Do the "Talk About" discussion questions now.)
1. Look at the giant cookie (before you cut it).
2. Help decorate the cookie.
3. Let the teacher cut the giant cookie into enough segments for everyone to have a piece.

Suggested Bible Stories
Abraham and the Three Visitors
David and Jonathan
A Widow Shares with Elijah
Elisha's Room on the Roof
Jesus Feeds 5,000

Talk About
• We have only one cookie. Who should get it? How can we all have some?
• You can share your food. What else can you share?
• Why does God want us to share?
• Who shared in our story? What did they share?

13

Honey Crunch Bananas

Ingredients
half of 1 banana for each child
honey
wheat germ

Kitchen Tools
plastic knives
baking sheet
paper plates
bowl
toothpicks

Guide Each Child To
1. Help spread wheat germ on the bottom of one baking pan.
2. Pour honey into the bowl.
3. Peel and slice her banana on her plate.
4. Stick a toothpick into a banana slice.
5. Dip the banana slice into honey and then roll it around in the wheat germ.
6. Do this with each banana slice.

Caution
Carefully supervise the children when using toothpicks

Suggested Bible Stories
Creation of People
Isaac Is Born
Birthright and Blessing
Joseph's Colorful Coat
Manna and Quail
Ravens Feed Elijah
Elisha's Room on the Roof
Jesus Feeds 5,000
Tax Money in a Fish
Jesus and the Children
Perfume on Jesus' Feet
Dorcas

Talk About
• Who gives us food to eat? That's one way God blesses us. Blessings are the good things that God gives us.
• How does this food taste? Is it crunchy? Is it soft?
• What part of your body tastes this food? Your tongue is one of the blessings God gives you.
• What part of your body smells this food? How does it smell? Your nose is one of the blessings God gives you.
• What other blessings has God given you? What was the blessing in our story?

Cooperation Cookies

Ingredients (for 2 children)
2 Tablespoons honey
2 Tablespoons peanut butter
1 cup crisp rice cereal

Kitchen Tools
disposable plastic bowls
waxed paper
measuring cups, spoons
paper plates
plastic spoons
paper towels

Guide Each Child To
1. Choose a friend to work with.
2. With her friend, get a bowl, a spoon, and a piece of waxed paper.
3. Work with her friend, mixing the honey and peanut butter in their bowl.
4. With her friend, add 1 cup crisp rice cereal and stir until the cereal is well coated.
5. Help her friend put spoonfuls of this mixture onto the waxed paper.
6. Help her friend get plates for their cookies.

Suggested Bible Stories
Creation of People
Ruth
David and Jonathan
Elijah Goes Up to Heaven
Daniel Refuses the King's Food
The Fiery Furnace
Jesus Chooses Twelve Friends
Through the Roof
Paul in a Basket
Timothy
Paul and Silas in Prison

Talk About
• How did you and your friend help each other? What are some other ways you can help your friends?
• Who are some of your friends?
• Who gives us good friends?
• Who were the good friends in our story? How did they help each other?

Heavenly Fruit Snack

Ingredients

3 teaspoons instant vanilla pudding mix for each child
1/4 cup milk for each child
graham cracker crumbs
frozen berries (strawberries or blueberries)
half of 1 banana for each child
1 can refrigerated whipped topping
1 maraschino cherry for each child

Kitchen Tools

measuring cups, spoons
plastic spoons, knives
paper plates
paper towels
bowl
paper cups
clear disposable cups

Prepare Ahead of Time

Thaw the frozen berries.

Guide Each Child To

1. Pour 1/4 cup milk into his paper cup.
2. Add pudding mix to his milk and stir well.
3. Peel and slice his half of banana on his plate.
4. Place one spoonful of his pudding into his clear cup.
5. On top of the pudding, put a spoonful of graham cracker crumbs, a spoonful of berries, and a few banana slices.
6. Squirt some whipped topping on the top.
7. Layer these same ingredients one more time and add a cherry on top.

Suggested Bible Stories

Elijah Goes Up to Heaven
The Lord's Prayer
The Wise Man's House
Jesus Goes Back to Heaven
John Sees Heaven

Talk About

• What is your favorite thing to eat?
• Some people say, "It's delicious!" Others say, "Mmmm! This is heavenly!" What do they mean? (it's wonderful)
• Name some things that you think are wonderful.
• Heaven is even more wonderful! What do you think heaven is like?

Egg Salad Sandwich

Ingredients
3 to 4 hard boiled eggs
1 to 2 Tablespoons chopped green olives
1 to 2 Tablespoons mayonnaise
bread

Kitchen Tools
knife for teacher
mixing spoon
cutting board
plastic knives
bowl
paper plates
fork
paper towels
measuring spoon

Prepare Ahead of Time
Boil the eggs, chop the green olives, and
cut each slice of bread in half.

Guide Each Child To
1. Help take the shells off the eggs and separate the yolks from the whites.
2. Mash the yolks in the bowl using the fork.
3. Add mayonnaise and olives and stir.
4. Watch the teacher chop the egg whites into small chunks.
5. Add he chopped egg whites to the yolk mixture and stir well.
6. Choose two half-slices of bread to put on her plate. Spread one piece of bread with the
   egg salad and top it with the other piece of bread.

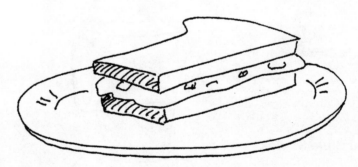

Suggested Bible Stories
Jacob's Dream
Baby Moses
Crossing the Red Sea
The Sun Stands Still
David and Goliath
Esther
The Fiery Furnace
Daniel and the Lions
Joseph, Mary, and Jesus Move to Egypt
Peter Escapes From Prison
Paul and Silas in Prison
Paul's Shipwreck

Talk About
• Why does an egg have a shell? What does
  the shell do for the egg? (protects the egg)
• What does protect mean?
• Who protects you? How does God protect
  you?
• Who protected the people in our story? What
  happened?

Peanut Butter

Ingredients
a few peanuts in the shell
2 cups roasted peanuts
1/2 teaspoon salt
1 Tablespoon peanut oil
crackers

Kitchen Tools
blender
paper plates
mixing bowl, spoon
paper towels
plastic knives
measuring cups, spoons

Guide Each Child To
1. Examine the peanuts in the shell and crack one open to see inside.
2. Help grind the peanuts in the blender, 1/2 cup at a time.
3. Put the ground peanuts in a bowl.
4. Stir in peanut oil and salt.
5. Put the peanut mixture back into the blender one cup at a time, adding a few drops of oil if necessary.
6. Blend the peanut mixture until smooth.
7. Spread the peanut butter on crackers.

Caution
Carefully supervise the children when using a blender

Variation: Bring boiled eggs in the shell and several peanuts in the shell. Give each child one boiled egg and a few peanuts. Help the children peel the eggs and peanuts. Slice the eggs for the children or let them bite into the eggs whole. Let the children dip their eggs in salt that you sprinkle onto their plates. Serve with juice.

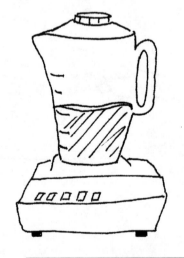

Suggested Bible Stories
Noah
Joseph Is Taken to Egypt
Baby Moses
Rahab and the Spies
David and Goliath
Esther
The Fiery Furnace
Daniel and the Lions
Jonah
The Lost Sheep
Paul in a Basket
Paul's Nephew Hears a Plot
Paul's Shipwreck

Talk About
• What covers the peanut while it's growing under the ground? (The shell protects the peanut.)
• How does the shell protect it? What does protect mean?
• Who protects you or takes care of you?
• Who protected the person in our story? What happened?

18

Tuna Salad

Ingredients
1 can of tuna
apple
dill or sweet pickles
mayonnaise
boiled egg
crackers

Kitchen Tools
knife
spoon, fork
can opener
bowl
paper towels

Prepare Ahead of Time
Boil the egg(s) and allow to cool.

Guide Each Child To
1. Let the teacher open the tuna can.
2. Let the teacher cut the apple, pickles, and egg into small pieces.
3. Taste some of each ingredient. (You might want them to close their eyes and guess what they're eating.)
4. Help mix all the ingredients in a bowl.
5. Help the teacher add enough mayonnaise to moisten the mixture.
6. Put some tuna salad on a cracker.

Suggested Bible Stories
Creation of People
Adam and Eve Eat the Fruit
Abraham and the Three Visitors
Birthright and Blessing
Manna and Quail
Twelve Spies
Ravens Feed Elijah
A Widow Shares With Elijah
Daniel Refuses the King's Food
John the Baptist
Birds and Flowers (Sermon on the Mount)
Jesus Feeds 5,000
Mary and Martha

Talk About
- How does the pickle taste? How does the apple taste? Does the egg taste like the apple?
- Does the tuna taste the same or different?
- The way things taste is called their flavor. Who made flavors?
- Who made mouths and tongues?
- Who tasted some flavors in our story? What happened?

Pita Pocket Message

Ingredients
pita bread

Kitchen Tools
knife
plastic sandwich bags

Prepare Ahead of Time
Write out the promise verses on slips of paper.

Guide Each Child To
1. Put her slip of paper into a sandwich bag.
2. Let the teacher cut each pita in half to make two pockets.
3. Slip her sandwich bag into a pita half.

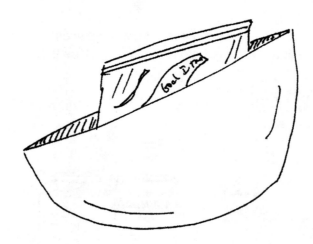

Promise Verses

Joshua 1:15	Psalm 25:12
Psalm 32:7, 8	Psalm 34:18, 22
Psalm 37:5, 6, 11	Psalm 37:18, 19
Psalm 37:23, 24	Psalm 37:27, 28
Psalm 41:1-3	Psalm 50:15
Psalm 55:22	Isaiah 1:18
Isaiah 41:10, 13	Isaiah 46:4
Isaiah 58:9	Isaiah 58:11
Isaiah 60:20	Isaiah 65:17
Matthew 7:7	Matthew 11:28, 29
Matthew 28;20	Mark 10:27
John 8:32	John11:25
John 14:12	John 14:14
John 14:27	John 16:13
John 16:24	Acts 1:11

Talk About
• What does the verse say?
• What does it mean?
• Who said it?
• Why is it important?

Cracker Fish in Soup

Ingredients
can of beef consommé or tomato soup
water
fish-shaped crackers

Prepare Ahead of Time
Heat soup and store in a thermos.

Guide Each Child To
1. Put several "fish" into his soup.
2. Eat soup and crackers.

Kitchen Tools
Styrofoam cups
paper towels
plastic spoons

Caution
Carefully supervise
the children when
eating hot soup

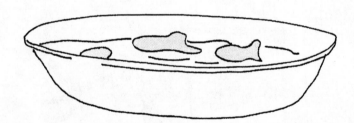

Suggested Bible Stories
Creation of Animals
Jonah
Jesus Chooses Twelve Friends
The Great Catch of Fish
The Fish and the Net
Jesus Feeds 5,000
Tax Money in a Fish
Jesus Makes Breakfast for His Friends

Talk About
• Where do fish live? What else lives in water?
• Name some different kinds of fish.
• Who made fish? Who made lakes and seas?
• What happened with fish in our story?

Peanut Butter Delight

Ingredients (for about 2 cups)
1 cup milk
2 teaspoons peanut butter
1/4 teaspoon honey
1/4 teaspoon vanilla
4 to 6 ice cubes
1 teaspoon sugar (optional)

Kitchen Tools
blender
measuring spoons, cups
paper cups
paper towels

Guide Each Child To
1. Help add the ingredients to the blender.
2. Let the teacher pour a small amount into a cup. Taste the drink.

Caution
Carefully supervise
the children when
eating hot soup

Suggested Bible Stories
Birthright and Blessing
Jesus Heals a Blind Man With Mud
Blind Bartimaeus
Paul to Damascus

Talk About
• We are mixing together some of God's gifts. What are they?
• Where does milk come from?
• Where does peanut butter come from?
• Where does honey come from?
• Where does vanilla come from?
• Would a person who is blind be able to enjoy this drink, even if he couldn't see it? Why?
• Could he tell what it was made of? How?
• Who was blind in our story? What happened?

Apricot Tea

Ingredients
one 18-ounce jar orange breakfast drink mix
1/4 cup sugar
1/2 cup pre-sweetened lemonade mix
1/2 cup instant decaffeinated tea
one 3-ounce package apricot gelatin
2 1/2 teaspoons cinnamon
1/2 teaspoon ground cloves
warm to hot water (in kettle or thermos)

Kitchen Tools
mixing bowl, spoon
measuring cups, spoons
Styrofoam cups
paper towels
paper or index cards
plastic bags
ribbon or yarn, hole punch

Prepare Ahead of Time
Heat the water. On the paper or index cards, copy these
directions (one card for each child):
Mix 1 1/2 to 2 Tablespoons of mix with
1 cup of hot water for each cup of Apricot Tea.

Caution
Carefully supervise
the children when
using hot water

Guide Each Child To
1. Take turns adding and helping mix the ingredients.
2. Put some tea mix in a plastic bag for her to take home and share.
3. Color the card and punch one hole it.
4. Help the teacher thread ribbon or yarn through the hold and tie it around the bag of tea mix.
5. Help make some tea to drink in class.

Suggested Bible Stories
Abraham and the Three Visitors
Ruth
David and Jonathan
A Widow Shares With Elijah
Elisha's Room on the Roof
Jesus Feeds 5,000
Mary and Martha
Bigger Barns

Talk About
• What kinds of food are the best for making a healthy body? Which are your favorite?
• Who planned for us to eat good foods?
• What does it mean to share? Who are you going to share your tea with?
• What are some reasons for giving to others?
• How does it feel when someone gives or shares with you?
• Who shared or gave in our story? What happened?

Candlesticks

Ingredients
half of 1 banana for each child
ready-made whipped topping
maraschino cherries (1 for each child)

Kitchen Tools
plastic spoons
paper plates
paper towels
knife to slice the bananas

Guide Each Child To
1. Let the teacher cut each banana in half.
2. Stand his half vertically on a plate. (You may need to cut both ends of each banana in order to balance the banana so it will stand.)
3. Spoon a small bit of whipped topping onto the top end of the banana.
4. Place a cherry on top of the whipped topping. The banana is the candle and the cherry is the flame.

Suggested Bible Stories
Creation of Light and Color
God Leads Israel With a Pillar of Fire
Gideon
Let Your Light Shine
The Lost Coin
John Sees Heaven

Talk About
• Who made light? Why do we need light?
• How do you get light in the daytime? How do you get light at night?
• Who saw light in our story? What happened?

Pineapple-Orange Whip

Ingredients (for 1 child)
1/4 cup cold pineapple juice
1/4 cup cold orange juice
1/4 cup cold skim milk
4 crushed ice cubes

Kitchen Tools
measuring cups
blender
paper cups

Prepare Ahead of Time
Multiply the measurements for the drink ingredients by the number of drinks you will need.

Caution
Carefully supervise the children when using a blender

Guide Each Child To
1. Help the teacher pour the ingredients into the blender.
2. Add ice cubes to the mixture.
3. Let the teacher blend the mixture until bubbly.

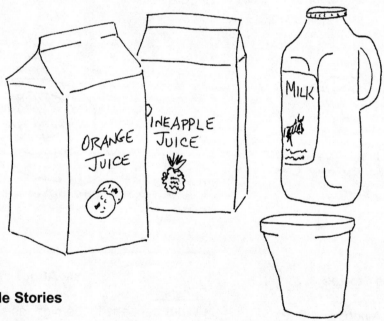

Suggested Bible Stories
Tower of Babel
Abraham and Lot
David and Jonathan
A Widow's Oil Jars
Rebuilding Jerusalem's Walls
Daniel Refuses the King's Food
Jesus Chooses Twelve Friends
Through the Roof
The Good Samaritan
Timothy
Paul and Silas in Prison

Talk About (as children make the drink)
• Talk about cooperation: one child adding something, one stirring, one measuring, and so on.
• Can you think of some things that are better done alone?
• What are some things that you have to do with others?
• How did God plan for friends to act toward each other?
• Did the people in the story cooperate or not? What happened?

Sunshine and Stars

Ingredients
* processed American cheese slices for "stars" OR
    boiled eggs for "sunshine"
round crackers

Kitchen Tools
knife for teacher
paper towels
paper plates
star-shaped cookie cutters

Prepare Ahead of Time
* Choose which activity goes best with your story selection. For _Sunshine_, boil the eggs and allow to cool. Slice the eggs into thin slices. Make enough for each child to try at least one egg sunshine. For _Stars_, use the star-shaped cookie cutter on the cheese slices. Do this in class and let the children help, if you have time. Make enough for each child to have at least one cheese star.

Guide Each Child To
1. Choose a "sunshine" egg (or cheese "star") and a cracker.
2. Place the egg slice (or cheese slice) on her cracker.

 OR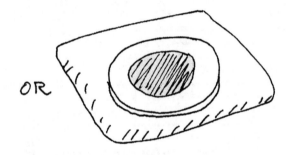

Suggested Bible Stories
Sunshine:
Creation of Sun, Moon, and Stars
Joseph's Dreams
The Sun Stands Still
John Sees Heaven
Stars:
Creation of Sun, Moon, and Stars
God's Promise to Abraham
Jacob's Dream
Joseph's Dreams
Jesus Is Born (the star over Bethlehem)
The Wise Men

Talk About
Sunshine:
• What happens to the night as soon as the sun starts coming up?
• Who made the sun?
• What was the light in our story? What happened?
Stars:
• Do you ever watch the sky at night? What do you see there?
• Who made the stars?
• Who saw the star(s) in our story. What happened?

Crunchy Chewies

Ingredients
1 cup peanut butter
1 cup instant dry milk
1/2 cup honey
crisp rice cereal

Kitchen Tools
measuring cups
mixing spoon
paper towels
waxed paper

Guide Each Child To
1. Help measure and mix the peanut butter, instant milk, and honey.
2. Roll a heaping teaspoonful of the mixture into a ball on waxed paper.
3. Roll the ball in the crisp rice cereal.

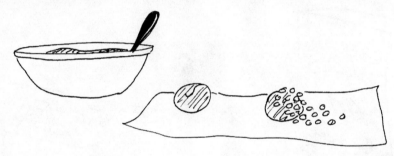

Suggested Bible Stories
Obeying:
Adam and Eve Eat the Fruit
Abraham Travels
Joseph in Prison
Joseph Leads Egypt
Crossing the Red Sea (Moses leads the Israelites)
The Ten Commandments
Balaam's Talking Donkey
Crossing The Jordan
Naaman
King Josiah Finds God's Word
The Wise Man's House
Two Sons and a Vineyard
Friends:
David and Jonathan
Elisha's Room on the Roof
The Fiery Furnace
Jesus Makes Breakfast for His Friends
Through the Roof
Jesus and the Children
Perfume on Jesus' Feet
Paul and Silas in Prison
Paul with Aquila and Priscilla

Talk About
Obeying:
• How did you obey? What would happen to our recipe if you didn't follow directions?
• Why must we obey our parents?
• Who obeyed in our story?
Friends:
• Sometimes friends eat together. What do you like to eat with your friends?
• How did you help each other make this snack?
• Friends help each others. Jesus is our best friend. How does he help us?
• Who were the friends in our story? What happened?

Hidden Treats

Ingredients

choose a snack which has a hidden treat inside
   (for example: peanut butter cups, chocolate treasure
   candies with caramel inside, yogurt-covered pretzels, etc)

Kitchen Tools

paper towels

Guide Each Child To

1. Help hand out a treats, one for each child.
2. Take time to examine the outside of the treat.
3. Break or bite open the treat to see what's inside.

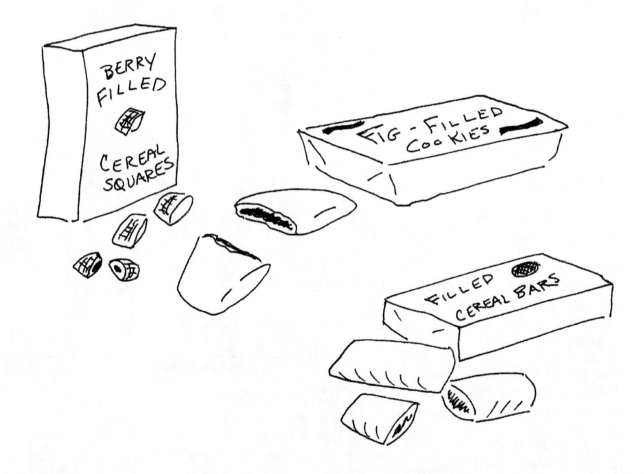

Suggested Bible Stories

King Josiah Finds God's Word
Tax Money in a Fish
Hidden Treasure
The Lost Coin

Talk About

• What was the outside of our treat made of? What was hidden inside?
• What was hidden in our story? Who found it?
• What kind of treasure does God want us to have?
• What was the treasure in our story? What happened?

Edible Map

Ingredients
fruit roll-ups

Kitchen Tools
paper plates
scissors for children*

Guide Each Child To
1. Take a paper plate and some fruit roll ups.
2. Tear the fruit roll-up into different shapes and lie them flat on his paper plate "globe." The roll-ups will be the "land" and the paper plate his "ocean."
3. Make "mountains" out of his fruit roll-ups.

*Note: Scissors are optional. If you choose to let children use scissors to cut shapes out of their roll-ups, be sure to wash the scissors throughly before using and supervise the children.

Suggested Bible Stories
Creation of Sky, Sea, and Land
Garden of Eden
Abraham and Lot
Twelve Spies
Israelites Wander in the Wilderness
Paul's Shipwreck

IDEA: This is also a good activity for the study of missions and missionaries.

Talk About
- Where is the "land" on your globe? Where is the "water" on your globe?
- How is an ocean different from mountains?
- Have you ever seen any mountains? An ocean? What were they like?
- What is the land like where you live?
- Who made the different land forms? How?
- Tell about the land (or ocean) in our story.

Peach Sherbet

Ingredients
? cup nonfat sour cream
2 Tablespoons plus 2 teaspoons sugar
2 teaspoons lemon juice
1 teaspoon vanilla
15 ounces frozen peaches

Kitchen Tools
small bowl
small paper cups
mixing spoon
plastic spoons
measuring cups, spoons
paper towels
blender

Guide Each Child To
1. Help mix the sour cream, sugar, lemon juice, and vanilla in the small bowl.
2. Crush the frozen peaches in the blender.
3. Add the sour cream mixture to the peaches and blend again.
4. Dip some of the sherbet into her cup.
5. Say a thank-you prayer to God before eating.

Caution
Carefully supervise the children when using a blender

Suggested Bible Stories
Isaac Gets a Wife
Hannah Prays for a Baby
David Plays the Harp
Daniel and the Lions
The Lord's Prayer
A Pharisee and a Tax Collector Pray
Paul and Silas in Prison

Talk About
• What is prayer? Where can we pray?
• Why do we pray before we eat? When are some other times we can pray?
• Who prayed in our story? What happened?

Mini Icees

Ingredients
ice
juice of your choice

Kitchen Tools
blender or ice crusher
long-handled mixing spoon
small paper cups
plastic spoons
paper towels

Prepare Ahead of Time
Freeze the ice or get a bag of ice at the grocery store.

Guide Each Child To
1. Help put ice into the blender.
2. Help crush the ice in the blender.
3. Add juice a little at a time to keep the mixture thick and icy.
4. Put a scoop of the flavored crushed ice into her cup.

Caution
Carefully supervise
the children when
using a blender

Suggested Bible Stories
Noah
The Plagues in Egypt (hail)
Jonah
Jesus Stills the Storm
Paul's Shipwreck

Talk About
• Sometimes ice comes down from the sky. What do we call it?
  (In warm weather, it's hail. In winter, it's sleet or snow.)
• Have you ever seen hail or sleet or snow? What was it like?
• Who made weather? What's your favorite weather?
• What was the weather like in our story?
• Who took care of the people in our story? Who takes care of you?

Cookie People

Ingredients

pre-made sugar cookies (or another type of cookie
    with a plain top), one for each child
decorator icing in a tube (several different colors)

Kitchen Tools

paper plates
paper towels

Guide Each Child To

1. Place a cookie on his plate.
2. Choose a tube of decorator icing and decorate his cookie with a face. Make eyes, nose, mouth, hair, ears, etc. (Let each child be creative in what he would like to include on his cookie face.)

Variation: Make Flower Cookies by letting the children use the decorator icing to draw flowers on the top of the cookie.

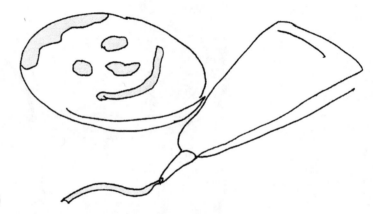

Suggested Bible Stories

People:
Creation of People
Twelve Spies (Joshua and Caleb)
Samson
Ruth
David and Mephibosheth
Naaman
John the Baptist
Jesus Chooses Twelve Friends
Through the Roof
Jesus Heals the Bent Woman
Ten Lepers
Zacchaeus
Flowers:
Creation of Plants
Garden of Eden
Aaron's Staff Blooms
Birds and Flowers (Sermon on the Mount)
Jesus in Gethsemane
The Resurrection (garden tomb)

Talk About

People:
• What did you put on your cookie face? Does your cookie face look like your friend's? How is it different? How is it the same?
• Who made people? How are you like other people? How are you different?
• How was the person in the story special or different? Did God still love him? What happened?
Flowers:
• Who made flowers?
• What kind of flower is your favorite?
• Tell about the flowers in our story. What happened?

Graham Cracker Goodies

Ingredients
graham crackers
ready-to-spread frosting
sugar sprinkles or candy sprinkles in a shaker

Kitchen Tools
plastic knives
poster board
marker
paper plates, towels

Prepare Ahead of Time
Make a rebus chart recipe on the poster board as shown.

Guide Each Child To
1. Follow the directions given on the rebus chart with as little help as possible.

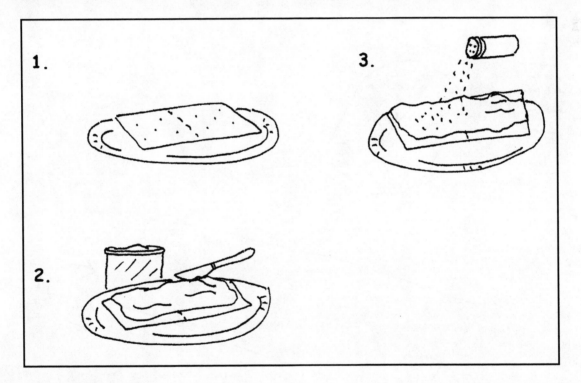

Suggested Bible Stories
Adam and Eve Eat the Fruit
The Ten Commandments
Crossing the Jordan
Jericho's Walls Fall Down
Naaman
King Josiah Finds God's Word
Jonah
Jesus Is Tempted
The Wise Man's House
Two Sons and a Vineyard

Talk About
• What would happen if you didn't follow the directions?
• What if you sprinkled salt instead of sugar?
• What if you didn't put frosting on the cracker first?
• What happens if we don't follow God's rules?
• Why does God have rules for us to obey?
• Did the people or person in our story obey or disobey? What happened?

Scroll Roll-Ups

Ingredients
fruit roll-ups, enough for each child to have one rectangle

Kitchen Tools
knife for teacher
paper plates
paper towels

Prepare Ahead of Time
Cut the fruit roll-ups into rectangles. (This can be done during class if you have time.)

Guide Each Child To
1. Place a fruit roll-up on her plate.
2. Roll up the two short sides so that they meet in the center as shown.

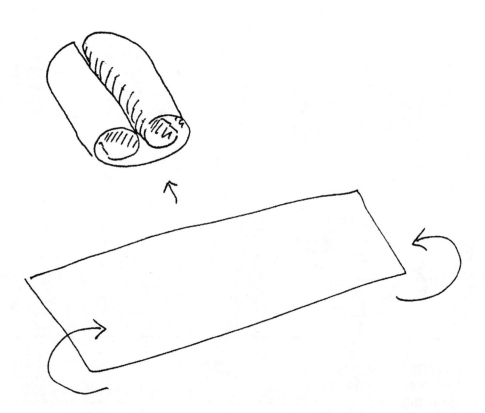

Suggested Bible Stories
King Josiah Finds God's Word
Jesus as a Boy in the Temple
Jesus Reads in the Synagogue
Philip and the Man From Ethiopia

Talk About
• What is a scroll?
• What was written on the scroll in our story? What happened?
• Where do we read God's words?

Fruit Punch

Ingredients
powdered, sweetened fruit punch mix
1 1/2 cups lemon-lime soda
1 quart of water
1 pint of orange or lime sherbet (optional)

Prepare Ahead of Time
Let the sherbet soften, but not melt.

Guide Each Child To
1. Help put the water into the pitcher.
2. Help add the amount of powdered mix recommended on the package to make 1 quart of punch.
3. Take turns stirring the drink mix into the water.
4. Help add 1 1/2 cups lemon-lime soda and stir.
5. Pour some of the punch into her cup.
6. Dip one small plastic spoonful of sherbet and add it to her cup of punch.

Kitchen Tools
pitcher
paper cups
long-handled spoon
plastic spoons
paper towels
dry measuring cups
measuring spoons
liquid measuring cups

Suggested Bible Stories
Esther
Writing on the Wall
Water Into Wine
The Runaway Son

Talk About
• People sometimes have punch like this at parties. Did you ever go to a party? What was it like?
• What was the party in our story?
• Why did they have the party? What happened?

Cloud Gelatin

Ingredients
2 1/2 cups boiling water
two 8-ounce packages of blue or purple gelatin mix
non-dairy whipped topping

Kitchen Tools
mixing bowl, spoon
scissors, knife
pancake turner
13 x 9-inch pan
baking sheet
paper plates
plastic spoons
paper towels
waxed paper

Prepare Ahead of Time
Mix the boiling water with the gelatin mix.
Pour into the pan and refrigerate at least 3 hours.
Dip the bottom of the pan into warm water for about 15
seconds. Draw a 3-inch wide cloud onto waxed paper.
Cut this out and use it as a pattern. Place the pattern
on the gelatin and cut around it. Cut out one cloud for each child. Lift the gelatin cloud out
of the pan and place it onto the baking sheet. Keep refrigerated until class time.

Guide Each Child To
1. Place a gelatin cloud on a paper plate.
2. Use his spoon to "frost" the cloud with the whipped topping.

Variation: See next page.

Suggested Bible Stories
Creation of Sky, Sea and Land
The Cloud Covers the Tabernacle
Elijah on Mt. Carmel (servant sees a cloud)
Jesus Goes Back to Heaven
John Sees Heaven

Talk About
• Who made clouds?
• What are clouds like?
• Tell about the cloud in the story. What
happened?

Gelatin Hearts

Ingredients
(see ingredient list on the previous page, substituting
   red gelatin for the blue or purple; omit whipped topping)

Kitchen Tools
(see tool list on the
   previous page)
heart-shaped cookie cutter

Prepare Ahead of Time
Follow the directions for making Cloud Gelatin listed on the previous page. Use a heart-shaped cookie cutter to cut the gelatin. If you have time, let the children help cut out the hearts. Do this activity with any of the praise stories listed below.

Guide Each Child To
1. Help cut out hearts from the gelatin.
2. Choose a gelatin heart and place on his paper plate.

Suggested Bible Stories
Crossing the Red Sea (Miriam's song of praise)
Deborah (after the battle)
David and Goliath
David Plays the Harp
Solomon (dedication of the temple)
Singers Lead Jehoshaphat's Army
Gabriel Appears to Mary (Mary's song of
praise)
The Triumphal Entry
Children Praise Jesus in the Temple
The Lost Coin

Talk About
• What does a heart make us think of? We
  think of love. Praising God is one thing
  that shows we love him.
• How can we praise God? What can we
  praise him for?
• When can we praise God?
• Who praised God in our story? How did
  they do it?

Cloud Pudding

Ingredients
instant chocolate pudding
milk
non-dairy whipped topping

Kitchen Tools
large bowl
long-handled spoon
small bowls
plastic spoons

Guide Each Child To
1. Help mix the instant chocolate pudding according to package directions.
2. Place a big spoonful of non-dairy whipped topping in their bowl.
3. Talk about how it looks like a cloud.
4. Place a small spoonful of chocolate pudding on top of the whipped topping.
5. Stir the pudding into the topping, making the topping dark.
6. Talk about how clouds get dark before it rains.

Suggested Bible Stories
Rain:
Noah
The Plagues in Egypt
Elijah on Mt. Carmel
Jonah
Jesus Stills the Storm
Jesus Walks on Water
The Wise Man's House
Paul's Shipwreck
Clouds:
Creation of Sky, Sea and Land
The Cloud Covers the Tabernacle
Elijah on Mt. Carmel (servant sees a cloud)
Jesus Goes Back to Heaven
John Sees Heaven

Talk About
Rain:
• Who makes rain?
• What kinds of animals like rain?
• What do you like about rain?
• What is a storm like?
• Who saw the storm in our story? How did God take care of them?
Clouds:
• Who made clouds?
• What are clouds like?
• Tell about the cloud in the story. What happened?

Waves on a Bagel

Ingredients
cream cheese
blue food coloring
half a bagel for each child

Kitchen Tools
knife for teacher
plastic spoon

Prepare Ahead of Time
Slice the bagels in half.

Guide Each Child To
1. Help mix blue food coloring into the cream cheese.
2. Put some cream cheese onto the bagel and make peaks in the cream cheese like waves.

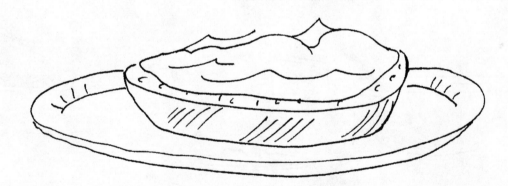

Suggested Bible Stories
Noah
Elijah on Mt. Carmel
Jonah
Jesus Stills the Storm
Jesus Walks on Water
The Wise Man's House
Paul's Shipwreck

Talk About
• Did you ever ride in a boat? What was it like?
• What happens to waves during a storm?
• Who was in a storm in our story? What did God do?
• How does God take care of you?

Fruit Yogurt Sundaes

Ingredients
one 8-ounce container of vanilla yogurt
1 Tablespoon of lemon or orange gelatin mix
1 can mandarin oranges
2 bananas
1 cup grapes
1/4 teaspoon cinnamon

Kitchen Tools
large and small mixing bowls
knife, mixing spoons
plastic bowls, spoons
can opener
measuring spoons
paper towels

Prepare Ahead of Time
Open the can of mandarin oranges. Just before the activity, slice the bananas into a small plastic bowl.

Guide Each Child To
1. Help stir 1 Tablespoon of gelatin mix into the yogurt in the small mixing bowl.
2. Help put the oranges, bananas, grapes, and cinnamon into the large mixing bowl. Take a turn stirring the fruit.
3. Put a big spoonful of fruit into his bowl.
4. Place a small spoonful of yogurt mixture on top.

Suggested Bible Stories
Adam and Eve Eat the Fruit
Abraham and the Three Visitors
Birthright and Blessing
Joseph's Brothers Go to Egypt
Twelve Spies
Manna and Quail
Abigail Packs Food
A Widow Shares with Elijah
John the Baptist (locusts and honey)
The Lord's Supper
Jesus Feeds 5,000
Jesus Makes Breakfast for His Friends

Talk About
• What kind of fruit do you like best?
• Who made fruit?
• What kind of food did the people in our story eat? What happened?

Rainbow Sandwiches

Ingredients
bread
cream cheese, softened
food coloring (four colors)

Kitchen Tools
four small plastic bowls
spoons
plastic knives
sharp knife for teacher
paper plates
paper towels

Prepare Ahead of Time
Cut the crusts off of the bread. Soften the cream cheese. Divide the cream cheese evenly among four bowls, one bowl for each color of food coloring.

Guide Each Child To
1. Help put food coloring in the bowls of cream cheese and take turns stirring it until the color is blended in.
2. Spread one slice of bread with one color of cream cheese.
3. Stack his slice of bread on top of slices that other children have spread with the other three colors. (When each child does this, there will be several four-layer sandwiches.)
4. Let the teacher cut across each sandwich to make four square sandwiches.
5. Place his sandwich on his plate and eat it.

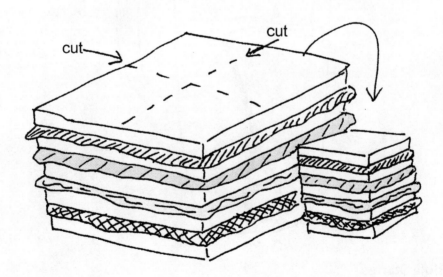

cut

cut

Suggested Bible Stories
Creation of Light and Color
Noah
Joseph's Colorful Coat
Birds and Flowers (Sermon on the Mount)
John Sees Heaven

Talk About
• Where would we look to see a rainbow?
• Who makes rainbows? What are some of the colors in rainbows?
• What was colorful in our story? What happened?

41

Lemonade

Ingredients
5 medium-sized lemons
5 cups cold water
1 cup sugar
optional: crackers

Kitchen Tools
knife for teacher's use
pitcher
measuring cups, spoons
long-handled spoon
paper cups
paper towels

Guide Each Child To
1. Watch as the teacher cuts the lemons so that each child can have part of a lemon.
2. Squeeze his part of the lemon into the pitcher.
3. Help add water and sugar.
4. Take a turn stirring the mixture.

Suggested Bible Stories
Water From a Rock
Ravens Feed Elijah
Daniel Refuses the King's Food
Writing on the Wall
Water Into Wine
The Lord's Supper
The Woman at the Well

Talk About
• What is your favorite thing to drink?
• How do you know when you need a drink?
• What did the people in our story drink? What happened?

Storm Soup

Ingredients
beef of chicken consommé or bouillon
croutons

Kitchen Tools
bowls
plastic spoons
paper towels

Prepare Ahead of Time
Heat the soup and store in a thermos.

Caution
Carefully supervise the children when eating hot soup

Guide Each Child To
1. Help pour some soup into his bowl.
2. Place several croutons on top of his soup and pretend these are boats.
3. Blow gently on the soup to make waves, then stir it to make a storm. Watch the "boats" toss up and down.
4. Eat the soup and croutons.

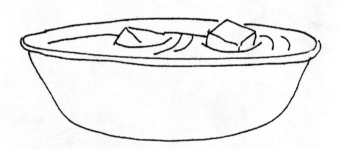

Suggested Bible Stories
Noah
Jonah
Jesus Stills the Storm
Jesus Walks on Water
Paul's Shipwreck

Talk About
• Have you ever been in a storm? What happened?
• Who takes care of you during a storm?
• Who was in a storm in our story? What happened?

Log House

Ingredients
cans of processed cheese
large, crunchy breadsticks or large pretzel rods

Kitchen Tools
waxed paper
aluminum foil
paper towels

Guide Each Child To
1. Divide into small groups.
2. As a group, take turns squirting a square outline of cheese on a piece of waxed paper.
3. Lay down the breadstick logs on the cheese outline.
4. Squirt more cheese on top of the logs and lay more breadsticks on top.
5. Add an aluminum foil roof.

Suggested Bible Stories
Rahab and the Spies
Solomon Builds the Temple
Elisha's Room on a Roof
The Wise Man's House

Talk About
• What is your house made of? Is the place where you live like other places in your neighborhood?
• Who gave us a place to live?
• Tell about the place to live in our story.

Graham Cracker House

Ingredients
graham crackers, four squares for each child
ready-to-spread frosting
candy (optional)

Kitchen Tools
paper plates
plastic knives or spoons
paper towels

Guide Each Child To
1. Take a paper plate and four squares of graham crackers.
2. Using the frosting as "glue," put three graham crackers together as walls to make a triangular house.
3. Spread frosting between the crackers at the corners to keep the house together.
4. Spread frosting across the top edges of the walls and place the square roof on top of these.
5. (Optional) Make doors, windows, and shingles on the roof by "gluing" candy to the house.

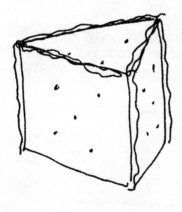
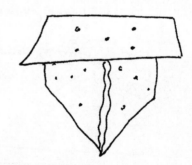

Suggested Bible Stories
Rahab and the Spies
Solomon Builds the Temple
Elisha's Room on a Roof
The Wise Man's House

Talk About
• Does the place where you live look like this one? Would you like to live in a house that looked like this? What does the place where you live look like?
• Are you the only one who lives in your room or do you share your room with someone else in your family?
• Who gives us a place to live?
• Tell about the place to live in our story.

Bird Nest Treats

Ingredients
two packages of butterscotch bits
chow mein noodles
peanuts
jelly beans

Kitchen Tools
waxed paper
plastic spoons
paper towels
microwave or stove

Prepare Ahead of Time
Do this just before starting this activity. Melt the butterscotch bits in a pan on the stove or in a microwave. (Stir frequently while butterscotch bits are melting to avoid overheating.) When melted, stir in one can of chow mein noodles and one can of peanuts.

Guide Each Child To
1. Take a square of waxed paper and a plastic spoon.
2. Being careful not to touch the hot mixture, drop a heaping teaspoonful of the mixture onto her wax paper.
3. Use the spoon to mash down the middle of the mixture to make a bowl-shaped nest.
4. Let it cool.
5. Put some jelly beans in the nest for bird eggs.

Variation: For Christmas, follow the same directions as above. After making the bowl-shape in the center of the mixture, gently press a pretzel twist onto each end of the mixture to make a manger. The pretzels form the manger legs. Omit the jelly beans.

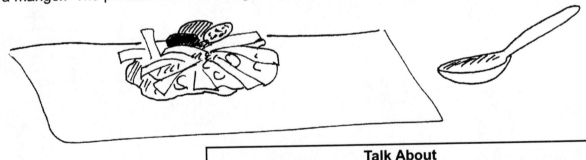

Suggested Bible Stories
Rahab and the Spies
Solomon Builds the Temple
Elisha's Room on a Roof
The Wise Man's House
For Christmas:
Jesus Is Born

Talk About
• Have you ever seen a birdhouse that someone built? What was it like?
• What does the place where you live look like? What color is it?
• What part of your house do you like the best?
• Who gives us a place to live?
For Christmas ask:
• Why did Joseph and Mary have to stay in a stable?
• What is a manger? Why did Mary put baby Jesus in a manger?
• Who came to see the baby? How did they know about him? Who was baby Jesus?

Guess the Food

Ingredients
various types of food with different flavors and textures, such as:
- sweet pickle • dill pickle
- apple • raisin
- peppermint candy
- potato chip or pretzel
- unsweetened chocolate
- cheese

Kitchen Tools
paper plates
paper towels
knife for teacher

Prepare Ahead of Time
Cut foods into bite-size pieces and place them on a plate.

Guide Each Child To
1. Close her eyes and open her mouth so she can guess what kind of food you will give them.
2. Allow the teacher to place a small bite of food on her tongue.
3. Taste the food and guess what it was.

Suggested Bible Stories
Manna and Quail
Abigail Packs Food
Ravens Feed Elijah
John the Baptist
Jesus Makes Breakfast for His Friends
Jesus Feeds 5,000

Talk About
• What does this taste like? Have you tasted it before? Where?
• Is it salty, sweet, sour, or bitter?
• Is it crunchy or soft and chewy?
• What is your favorite food?
• Who gives us food to eat?

Veggies and Dip

Ingredients

variety of fresh vegetables such as:
- carrots
- celery
- zucchini
- broccoli
- cauliflower
- vegetable dip

Kitchen Tools

knife for teacher
large plastic bag
paper plates
paper towels
small bowl, spoon

Prepare Ahead of Time

Wash and dry the vegetables and cut them into bite size pieces.
Place the veggies in a large plastic bag and mix them together.
Put vegetable dip in a serving bowl.

Guide Each Child To

1. Spoon a portion of the veggie mix onto his plate.
2. Separate the vegetables on his plate putting all the broccoli in one place, all the carrots in another, and so on. (This helps them learn to sort and classify.)
3. Spoon some dip onto his plate and eat his veggies and dip.

Suggested Bible Stories

Manna and Quail
Abigail Packs Food
Ravens Feed Elijah
John the Baptist
Jesus Makes Breakfast for His Friends
Jesus Feeds 5,000

Talk About
- What colors of vegetables do you have? Do they all
  taste alike?
- Which do you like best?
- Who gives us food to eat?
- Who had food in our story? What did they eat?

Flower Pops

Ingredients
4 cups miniature marshmallows
1/4 cup margarine
1/3 cup peanut butter
7 cups corn flakes cereal
cooking oil spray

Kitchen Tools
bowl for microwave
long-handled spoon
wood craft sticks
waxed paper
paper towels

Prepare Ahead of Time
To save time in class, pre-measure and store ingredients until ready to use.

Guide Each Child To

Caution
Carefully supervise the children as mixture will be hot.

1. Help mix the marshmallows and margarine together in a microwave safe bowl.
2. Help put the mixture in the microwave to melt. Let the teacher set it on high for 1 1/2 minutes, stir and continue heating for 1 1/2 minutes longer.
3. Help stir in the peanut butter and corn flakes.
4. Take her craft stick and swirl it in the mixture, scooping some on the end of her stick. (You may need to help with a spoon.)
5. Set the snack-on-a-stick on waxed paper that's been sprayed with cooking oil spray. Let it cool.
6. Pretend that the stick is the stem and the snack is the flower.

Suggested Bible Stories
Creation of Plants
Garden of Eden
Aaron's Staff Blooms
Birds and Flowers (Sermon on the Mount)
Jesus in Gethsemane
The Resurrection (garden tomb)

Talk About
• Where have you seen real flowers growing?
• What is your favorite color of flower?
• Who made flowers?
• Can we eat real flowers?
• Tell about the flowers in our story.

Cracker Flower

Ingredients
large, circle-shaped crackers (five crackers for each child)
processed canned cheese
oyster crackers

Kitchen Tools
paper plates
paper towels

Guide Each Child To
1. Put four crackers on her plate into a square shape.
2. Squirt processed canned cheese in the center.
3. Press another circular cracker on that.
4. Squirt more cheese in the center and press the smaller cracker on top.

Suggested Bible Stories
Creation of Plants
Garden of Eden
Aaron's Staff Blooms
Birds and Flowers (Sermon on the Mount)
Jesus in Gethsemane
The Resurrection (garden tomb)

Talk About
• Who made flowers and plants?
• Who saw the plants in our story? What happened?
• What kind of plants do you like?

Bookwiches

Ingredients
cheese slices
bread slices

Kitchen Tools
knife for teacher
cookie cutters of different
   shapes

Prepare Ahead of Time
Trim the crusts off the bread slices.

Guide Each Child To
1. Use a cookie cutter to cut shapes out of the square cheese slices.
2. Places the cheese shapes between two pieces of bread.
3. Pretend these are books which they can open and see what's inside.
4. Tell the class what is inside his book.

Suggested Bible Stories
The Ten Commandments
King Josiah Finds God's Word
Ezra Reads God's Words
Jesus Reads in the Synagogue

Talk About
• Show a Bible and say, "This is a real book."
  What's inside?
• Open the Bible and read, "God is great. God
  is good. God is love."
• What is your favorite story in the Bible?
• When do you open your own Bible at home?
• What do you see inside? What does the
  Bible tell you?

Cheese-in-Betweens

Ingredients
American cheese slices
saltine crackers

Kitchen Tools
knife for teacher

Prepare Ahead of Time
Cut American cheese slices into smaller squares that will fit on a square saltine cracker.

Guide Each Child To
1. Take two crackers and put one on top of the other.
2. Notice that one cracker is on the top and one cracker is on the bottom.
3. Take a cheese slice and put it "in between" the crackers.

1. Two crackers -- nothing "in-between."

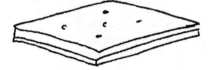

2. Put cheese "in-between"

Suggested Bible Stories
The Ten Commandments
King Josiah Finds God's Word
Ezra Reads God's Words
Jesus Reads in the Synagogue

Talk About
• Lay a Bible on the table. Touch the top cover gently. Say, "This is the top."
• Point to the bottom cover and say, "This is the bottom."
• What's in between?
• What does the Bible tell us about God?

Animal Crackers

Ingredients
animal crackers
peanut butter*

Kitchen Tools
paper plates
paper towels
plastic spoons

* If any child is allergic to peanuts, you may use
  ready made frosting or cream cheese.

Guide Each Child To
1. Put several animal crackers on his paper plate.
2. Let the teacher put a dab of peanut butter on his plate.
3. Use his spoon to frost his animal crackers with peanut butter.

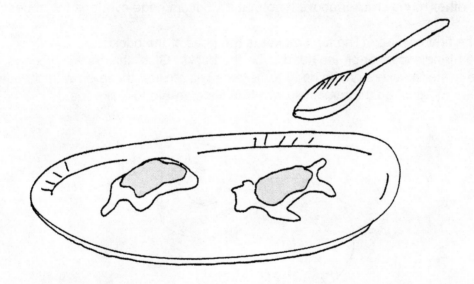

Suggested Bible Stories
Creation of Animals
Adam Names the Animals
Noah
Rebekah Gives Water to the Camels
Rachel's Sheep
Balaam's Talking Donkey
Saul Looks for Lost Donkeys
Solomon Knows About Animals
Ravens Feed Elijah
Daniel and the Lions
The Lost Sheep

Talk About
• What kind of animal cracker do you have?
• What sound does that animal make?
• How does it move around?
• Who made animals?
• Which kind of animal is your favorite?
• Tell about the animal(s) in our story.

53

Cracker Duck

Ingredients
large round crackers (two for each child)
small triangle-shaped crackers (three for each child)
oyster crackers (two for each child)
canned processed cheese

Kitchen Tools
paper plates
paper towels

Guide Each Child To
1. Take a paper plate, two large round crackers, three small triangle-shaped crackers and two small round oyster crackers.
2. Watch the teacher as she demonstrates how to make a duck with the crackers. (See illustration)
3. Squirt processed canned cheese onto the top edge of one round cracker.
4. Place the other round cracker above it so that it's bottom edge overlaps the cheese on the top
   edge of the first cracker. (The top cracker is the head of the duck.)
5. Place one triangle cracker on the head to be the beak. "Glue" this on with cheese.
6. Place two oyster crackers on the head to be the eyes. "Glue" these on with cheese.
7. Use cheese to "glue" on the remaining two triangle crackers to make feet.

Suggested Bible Stories
Creation of Animals
Adam Names the Animals
Noah
Rebekah Gives Water to the Camels
Rachel's Sheep
Balaam's Talking Donkey
Saul Looks for Lost Donkeys
Solomon Knows About Animals
Ravens Feed Elijah
Daniel and the Lions
The Lost Sheep

Talk About
• Who made ducks?
• What sound do ducks make? How do they move around?
• Where have you seen ducks before?
• What other animals did God make?
• Tell about the animal(s) in our story.

Bananapillars

Ingredients
one-half of a banana for each child
peanut butter

Kitchen Tools
wooden craft stick
paper plates
paper towels

Guide Each Child To
1. Take a paper plate, a craft stick and one-half of a banana.
2. Let the teacher help her slice the banana into several round pieces.
3. Use the craft stick top each banana piece with peanut butter.
4. Stick the round pieces together to make one banana "caterpillar."

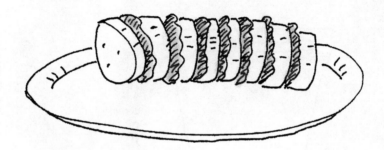

Suggested Bible Stories
Animals:
Creation of Animals
Adam Names the Animals
Noah
Rebekah Gives Water to the Camels
Rachel's Sheep
Balaam's Talking Donkey
Saul Looks for Lost Donkeys
Solomon Knows About Animals
Ravens Feed Elijah
Daniel and the Lions
The Lost Sheep
Growing Up:
Samuel's New Coats
Joash, Boy King
Josiah, Boy King
Jesus as a Boy in the Temple

Talk About
Animals:
• Have you ever seen a caterpillar?
• Who made caterpillars?
• What other kinds of animals did God make?
• Which kind is your favorite?
Growing Up:
• What does a caterpillar grow up to be? What will you grow up to be?
• Who makes you grow?
• How can we serve God as we grow up?

Trail Mix

Ingredients
raisins
plain granola or small donut-shaped cereal
peanuts*
sunflower seeds

Kitchen Tools
small paper cups

* If any child is allergic to peanuts, you may use pretzels.

Guide Each Child To
1. Put a little of each ingredient into her cup and mix it up.
2. As a group, take a pretend hike indoors or a real hike outside to a location where she can snack on her trail mix.

Suggested Bible Stories
Abraham Travels
Jacob's Family (traveling)
Joseph is Taken to Egypt
Joseph's Brothers Go to Egypt
God Leads Israel With a Pillar of Fire
Israelites Wander in the Wilderness
Naaman
Servant Sees God's Army
The Fiery Furnace
Joseph, Mary and Jesus Move to Egypt
The Good Samaritan
The Runaway Son
Philip and the Man From Ethiopia
Paul to Damascus

Talk About
• Let's pretend to follow a trail. We have our trail mix to eat when we get to a good place.
• If we take the trail to the beach, is God with us there?
• If we take the trail to the lake, is God with us there?
• If we take the trail into the big city, is God with us there?
• Who was God with in our story? What happened?

Bus Cookies

Ingredients
rectangular graham crackers (one for each child)
vanilla wafers (two for each child)
square-shaped cereal (3 to 4 for each child)
ready-to-spread frosting

Kitchen Tools
paper plates
paper towels
plastic knife or spoon

Guide Each Child To
1. Put his graham cracker on his paper plate.
2. Place two dots of frosting along the bottom of the graham cracker.
3. Press two vanilla wafers onto the frosting to make bus wheels.
4. Place several dots of frosting on the graham cracker where windows would be on a bus.
5. Press several pieces of square-shaped cereal on the frosting to make bus windows.

Suggested Bible Stories
Abraham Travels
Jacob's Family (traveling)
Joseph is Taken to Egypt
Joseph's Brothers Go to Egypt
Israelites Wander in the Wilderness
Naaman
Servant Sees God's Army
The Fiery Furnace
Joseph, Mary and Jesus Move to Egypt
The Good Samaritan
The Runaway Son
Philip and the Man From Ethiopia
Paul to Damascus

Talk About
• Did you ever ride the bus? Where did you go? What did you see?
• Did God go with you?
• Who was God with in our story?
• How did God take care of them?

Chariot Wheels

Ingredients
round crackers
canned processed cheese

Kitchen Tools
paper plates
paper towels

Guide Each Child To
1. Place his crackers on the paper plate.
2. Squirt processed cheese from a can onto the crackers in lines that look like spokes. (You may need to demonstrate and help the children.)

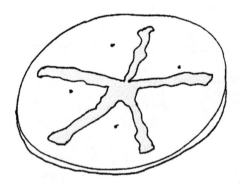

Suggested Bible Stories
Abraham Travels
Jacob's Family (traveling)
Joseph is Taken to Egypt
Joseph's Brothers Go to Egypt
Israelites Wander in the Wilderness
Naaman
Servant Sees God's Army
The Fiery Furnace
Joseph, Mary and Jesus Move to Egypt
The Good Samaritan
The Runaway Son
Philip and the Man From Ethiopia
Paul to Damascus

Talk About
• These look like wheels. Name something that has wheels.
• What do you like to ride in? Where do you like to go?
• How else could you get from one place to another?
• Does God go with you? God will never leave you.
• Who was God with in our story?
• How did God take care of them?

Popcorn Praise

Ingredients
popcorn for microwave or hot air popper

Kitchen Tools
microwave or hot air popper
paper towels or bowls

Guide Each Child To
1. Sit quietly on the floor while the teacher pops the popcorn.
2. Listen quietly for the popcorn to start popping.
3. Start jumping, clapping and praising God when the popping starts.
4. Sit down quietly when the popping stops.
5. Eat the popcorn while the teacher talks with the class.

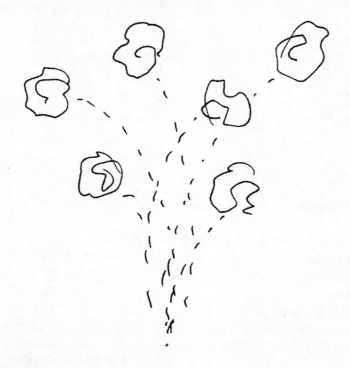

Suggested Bible Stories
Crossing the Red Sea (Miriam's song of praise)
Deborah (after the battle)
David and Goliath
David Plays the Harp
Solomon (dedication of the temple)
Singers Lead Jehoshaphat's Army
Gabriel Appears to Mary (Mary's song of praise)
The Triumphal Entry
Children Praise Jesus in the Temple
The Lost Coin

Talk About
• What is praise?
• What are some ways we can praise God?
• What do you want to praise him for right now?
• Who praised God in our story?
• How did they praise God?

Praise Pudding

Ingredients
large instant vanilla pudding
milk
one-half a banana for each child
vanilla wafers

Kitchen Tools
a quart jar with lid
plastic knife
paper cups or bowls
paper towels

Guide Each Child To
1. Help put the pudding mix into the jar and add milk. Place the lid on the jar and take turns shaking the pudding to mix it. Listen to the shaking sound of the pudding.
2. Help slice his half a banana into his cup and add vanilla wafers and pudding to the cup.

Suggested Bible Stories
Praise:
Crossing the Red Sea (Miriam's song of praise)
Deborah (after the battle)
David and Goliath
David Plays the Harp
Solomon (dedication of the temple)
Singers Lead Jehoshaphat's Army
Gabriel Appears to Mary (Mary's song of praise)
The Triumphal Entry
Children Praise Jesus in the Temple
The Lost Coin
Family:
Adam and Eve Have a Family
Isaac Is Born
Jacob and Esau
Joseph's Brothers Go to Egypt
Baby Moses
Rahab and the Spies (Rahab saves her family)
Ruth
David is Anointed (Jesse and sons)
Joseph, Mary and Jesus Move to Egypt

Talk About
Praise:
• What is praise? When can we praise God? Where can we praise God?
• Can we praise God while we're making pudding?
• What can we praise God for?
• Who praised God in our story? What did they praise God for?
Family:
• How did you help make our snack?
• Who makes snacks for you at home? How do you help?
• How do your brothers and sisters help with snacks or meals?
• Do you and your brothers or sisters have a favorite snack?
• Do your parents have a favorite snack?
• Who made our families? Why did God give us families?
• Tell about the family in our story.

Veggie Faces

Ingredients
a variety of vegetables and fruits in bite-size pieces, such as:
- carrots in disks and sticks
- cherry tomatoes
- orange sections
- raisins
- olives
- grapes
- pineapple chunks

Kitchen Tools
paper plates
paper towels
tray

Prepare Ahead of Time
Prepare the vegetables and fruits and place them on a tray.

Guide Each Child To
1. Choose vegetables and fruits to put on her paper plate.
2. Use the vegetables and fruits to create faces on her plate.

Suggested Bible Stories
Samuel's New Coats
Joash, Boy King
Josiah, Boy King
Jesus as a Boy in the Temple

Talk About
- Do you have short hair or long hair? Will your hair grow too?
- How can you tell you are growing?
- Who makes your body grow?
- Who was growing in our story?

61

Fruit Salad

Ingredients

a variety of fresh fruits, such as:
- apples
- bananas
- raisins
- seedless grapes
- oranges

Kitchen Tools

knife for teacher
large bowl
small paper cups
paper towels

Prepare Ahead of Time

Wash and cut fruit into bite size pieces. (You can do this during class if you have time.)

Guide Each Child To

1. Help put the different fruits into a bowl and stir.
2. Use the paper cup to scoop out some fruit and eat it.

Suggested Bible Stories

Daniel Refuses the King's Food
The Woman at the Well (Jesus rests by the well)
Jesus Washes His Friends' Feet

Talk About
- Why are fruits and vegetables good for your body?
- What is your favorite fruit?
- What other foods are good for you?
- What did the people in the story do to stay healthy?

Peanut Honey Dip

Ingredients
1/2 cup peanut butter
1 Tablespoon honey
1 Tablespoon vegetable oil
1 Tablespoon of sunflower seeds
crackers

Kitchen Tools
measuring cups, spoons
mixing bowl
mixing spoon

Guide Each Child To
1. Help make the dip by placing all ingredients in the bowl.
2. Help mix the dip by stirring it together.
3. Dip her cracker into the dip and eat it.

Suggested Bible Stories
Adam and Eve Eat the Fruit
The Ten Commandments
Naaman
King Josiah Finds God's Word
Recab's Family
Jonah
Jesus Is Tempted
The Wise Man's House
Two Sons and a Vineyard

Talk About
• What happens if you don't follow the recipe?
• What if you put in ketchup instead of honey?
• Why is it important to follow directions and obey them?
• Who does God want us to obey? Why?
• Did the people in our story obey or disobey? What happened?

Vanilla Wafer Sandwiches

Ingredients
four vanilla wafers for each child
peanut butter*

Kitchen Tools
paper plates
paper towels
plastic spoon or knife

* If any child is allergic to peanuts, you may use
  ready-made frosting or cream cheese.

Guide Each Child To
1. Put four vanilla wafers on her paper plate.
2. Use a plastic spoon or knife to spread peanut butter on two of the cookies.
3. Place another cookie on top of the peanut butter.
4. Keep one cookie and give one to a friend in the group. (Every child shares, but still gets two cookies.)

Suggested Bible Stories
Abraham and the Three Visitors
Ruth
David and Jonathan
A Widow Shares With Elijah
Elisha's Room on the Roof
Jesus Feeds 5,000
Mary and Martha
Bigger Barns

Talk About
• Is it always easy to share?
• What do you share at home? What do you share in class?
• Why does God want us to share?
• What did the people in our story share?

Apple Cheesewiches

Ingredients
four large cheese crackers for each child
two thin slices of apple for each child

Kitchen Tools
knife for teacher
paper plates
paper towels

Prepare Ahead of Time
Peel and cut the apples into thin slices to easily fit on the cracker.

Guide Each Child To
1. Place four large cheese crackers on his plate and two thin slices of apple.
2. Make a sandwich by placing the apple between the cheese crackers.
3. Keep one cheesewich and give one to a friend in the group. (Every child shares, but still gets two cheesewiches.)

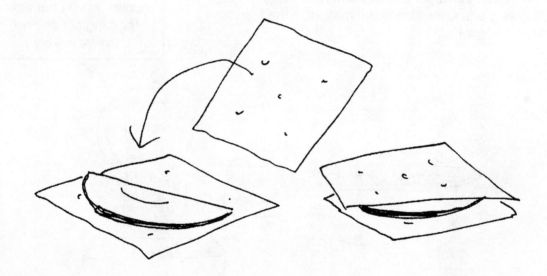

Suggested Bible Stories
Abraham and the Three Visitors
Ruth
David and Jonathan
A Widow Shares With Elijah
Elisha's Room on the Roof
Jesus Feeds 5,000
Mary and Martha
Bigger Barns

Talk About
• What does it mean to share? How does it feel when someone shares with you?
• Tell about a time when you shared your food.
• Why does God want us to share?
• Who shared in our story? What did they share?

Applesauce

Ingredients
four apples
2 tablespoons apple juice
? cup sugar
? teaspoon cinnamon

Prepare Ahead of Time
Peel and slice four apples.

Guide Each Child To
1. Help put the sliced apples in a large microwave-safe bowl.
2. Add the apple juice and cover the dish with plastic wrap.
3. Wait as the teacher puts the bowl in the microwave on high for six minutes.
4. Carefully add the sugar and cinnamon.
5. Watch as the teacher blends the mixture in the blender. (Serve it warm.)

Kitchen Tools
microwave and bowl
plastic wrap
long-handled spoon
blender
paper cups
plastic spoons
paper towels

Caution
Carefully supervise the children when using a blender.

Apples will be hot after coming out of the microwave.

Suggested Bible Stories
Joseph at Potiphar's House
Pharaoh's Dreams
Joseph Leads Egypt
Building the Tabernacle
Samuel's New Coats (helping Eli)
A Widow's Oil Jars
The Good Samaritan
The Lost Coin
Peter and John Heal a Lame Man
Dorcas

Talk About
• Who cooks at your house? Do you help? How?
• How did you help make our applesauce?
• What else do you do to help around your house?
• Who helped in our story?

Campfire Snack

Ingredients
Chex cereal
small pretzels
sunflower seeds

Kitchen Tools
large bowl
small paper cups
flashlight
wooden blocks (logs for a
    pretend fire)

Guide Each Child To
1. Help pour ingredients in a large bowl and mix together.
2. Fill her cup with the snack.
3. Help build a pretend fire on the floor by stacking blocks like logs.
4. Place a flashlight among the blocks and turn off the room light.
5. Sit around the "campfire" to eat the snack.

Suggested Bible Stories
God Talks to Isaac
Jacob's Dream
God Leads Israel With a Pillar of Fire
Jesus Is Born
Jesus in Gethsemane
Peter Escapes From Prison
Paul On Malta

Talk About
• Did you ever go camping? What was it like?
• Where did you sleep?
• Was God with you there?
• Does God sleep?
• How did God take care of the people in our
  story?

Birthday Cake

Ingredients
ready-made birthday cake*

Kitchen Tools
candles and matches
paper plates
paper towels
knife
plastic forks

Prepare Ahead of Time
Purchase a ready-made birthday cake from a bakery.
*If you have time you could bake your own and let
the children help decorate the cake.

Guide Each Child To
1. Look at the birthday cake and talk about his birthday memories. (Have the discussion time now before proceeding.)
2. After the discussion, help place candles on the cake.
3. Help cut the cake and eat it.

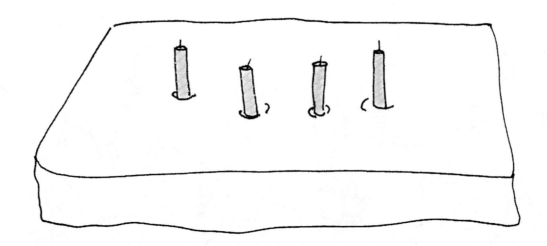

Suggested Bible Stories
Gabriel Appears to Mary
Jesus Is Born
Angels Appear to the Shepherds
The Wise Men

Talk About
• What is a birthday?
• What did you do on your birthday?
• What is your favorite part of a birthday?
• When were you born?
• Who was born in Bethlehem in a stable? Who came to see him?
• Who is baby Jesus?
• When we have Christmas, we celebrate Jesus' birthday.

Red Cross Muffins

Ingredients
ready-made muffins, any flavor*
red decorator frosting in a tube

Kitchen Tools
paper towels
paper plates

*You may substitute English muffins or biscuits and use red jelly in a squirt bottle instead of frosting

Guide Each Child To
1. Place a muffin on her paper plate.
2. Use the tube of frosting to make a large red cross on top of her muffin. (You will need to demonstrate how to do this.)

Suggested Bible Stories
Naaman
Through the Roof
The Lame Man at the Pool
The Centurion's Sick Servant
Woman Touches Jesus' Hem
Ten Lepers
Jesus Heals the Bent Woman
The Man's Withered Hand
Peter and John Heal a Lame Man

Talk About
• Have you ever seen something with a big red cross on it?
• What does the red cross mean?
• How can you help people who are sick?
• Who was sick in our story? What happened?

Graham Cracker Stable

Ingredients
frosting
graham crackers
miniature marshmallows

Kitchen Tools
paper plates
paper towels
large bowl
stickers of Mary, Joseph,
and baby Jesus

Caution
Carefully supervise
the children when
using candles.

Prepare Ahead of Time
Make your own frosting "glue" at home by mixing together 1/2 pound of powdered sugar, 2 egg whites (at room temperature), and 1/4 teaspoon of cream of tartar. Blend, then beat at high speed for 7-10 minutes. If you make the frosting ahead of time, store it in a tightly covered container and keep it refrigerated. It dries quickly and dries hard.

Guide Each Child To
1. Take a paper plate and three graham crackers.
2. Dip the crackers in the frosting just enough to get frosting on the edges.
3. Arrange the crackers as shown and hold them for a minute while the frosting hardens.
4. Use the frosting to glue the miniature marshmallows (sheep) on the floor of this "stable."
5. Glue Mary, Joseph, and baby Jesus stickers on the floor of the stable in the same way so that they are standing.

Variation: See next page.

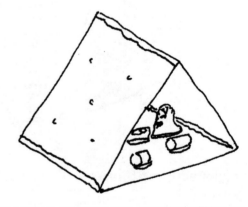

Suggested Bible Stories
Gabriel Appears to Mary
Jesus Is Born
Angels Appear to the Shepherds
The Wise Men

Talk About
• What is a stable? Why did Mary and Joseph have to stay in a stable?
• What is a manger? Why did Mary put baby Jesus in a manger?
• Who came to see the baby?
• Who is baby Jesus?

70

Graham Cracker Toy Box

Ingredients
(see ingredient list on the previous page,
   substitute animal graham crackers for marshmallows)

Kitchen Tools
(see tool list on the
   previous page)
omit stickers

Prepare Ahead of Time
Follow the directions on the previous page for making the "glue" frosting. Increase
ingredients to 3 egg whites, ? tsp cream of tartar, 1 pound powdered sugar. Use four full-
size graham crackers for each child and animal crackers.

Guide Each Child To
1. Dip the edges of his graham crackers in the frosting.
2. Make a rectangle by placing one long graham cracker on the bottom and one long
   graham cracker on each side.
3. Break the last graham cracker in half to make the sides of the toy box.
4. Place animal crackers inside the toy box.

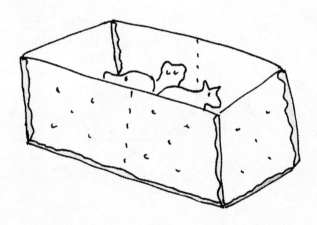

Suggested Bible Stories
Joseph at Potiphar's House
Taking Care of the Worship House
Good, Wise People
The Lost Coin

Talk About
• How do people keep rooms clean and neat?
• How do you take care of your room? Why?
• Do you have a toy box to keep all your toys in?
• How did the people in the story take care of their
  places?

Noisy Foods

Ingredients
celery sticks
carrot sticks
apple slices
saltine crackers
peanuts*
chow mein noodles

Kitchen Tools
paper towels

* If any child is allergic to peanuts, you may use pretzels.

Prepare Ahead of Time
Wash and cut the veggies and fruit into bite-size slices.

Guide Each Child To
1. Listen to the sounds the different foods make as he eats it.

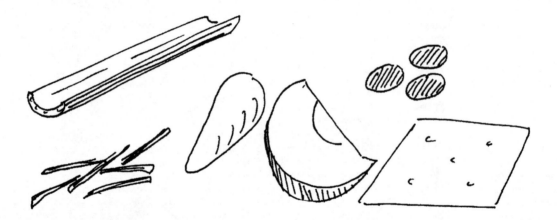

Suggested Bible Stories
Birthright and Blessing
God Talks to Isaac
Burning Bush
Samuel Hears God
David Listens for the Sound of Marching
The King Burns the Scroll
Jesus as a Boy in the Temple
The Wise Man's House
The Sower and the Seeds
Mary and Martha
Blind Bartimaeus
Peter and Cornelius
Paul's Nephew Hears a Plot

Talk About
• What are some other foods that are noisy?
• What are some foods that are quiet?
• What's your favorite food?
• Who does God want us to listen to? Why?
• Who listened (or didn't listen) in our story? What did he or she hear?

Worm Farm

Ingredients
instant chocolate pudding
milk
graham cracker crumbs
gummy worms

Kitchen Tools
large bowl
long-handled spoon
small bowls
plastic spoons
paper towels

Guide Each Child To
1. Help the teacher make instant chocolate pudding.
2. Place a small amount of pudding in her bowl.
3. Sprinkle some graham cracker crumbs on top of her pudding.
4. Put gummy worms on top of their "dirt."

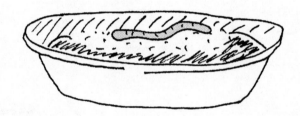

Suggested Bible Stories
Pets:
Rebekah Gives Water to the Camels
Rachel's Sheep
Balaam's Talking Donkey
The Lost Sheep
Land:
Creation of Land, Sea, and Sky
Abraham and Lot (Lot chooses land)
Israelites Wander in the Wilderness

Talk About
Pets:
• Some people have bugs or worms for pets. How would you take care of bugs or worms?
• What other animals are good pets?
• How were the people in our story kind to animals?
Land:
• This looks like dirt, but is it really dirt?
• What do you find when you dig in the dirt?
• Who made the dirt?

73

Banana Peach Sparkle

Ingredients
two peaches
two bananas
carbonated lemon-lime canned drink

Kitchen Tools
blender
knife for teacher
small paper cups
plastic spoons
paper towels

Prepare Ahead of Time
Peel and slice two peaches. Keep the peach skin for discussion.

Caution
Carefully supervise the children when using a blender

Guide Each Child To
1. Help place chunks of the sliced peaches in a blender.
2. Help peel two bananas, break them into pieces, and put them in a blender.
3. Watch as the teacher blends the two fruits together.
4. Put a few spoonfuls of the fruit mixture into her cup.
5. Let the teacher pour some lemon-lime canned drink on top of the fruit mix until the cup is three-fourths full.
6. Stir gently with a spoon before drinking.

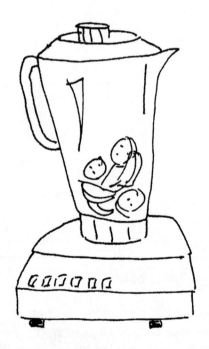

Suggested Bible Stories
Adam's Job
Bitter Water Turns Sweet
David Sings
Jesus Feeds 4,000 (Jesus' friends picked up leftovers)

Talk About
• What do we have left that we can't eat? (Banana peel, peach skin, cans from the lemon-lime drink.)
• What do we need to do with these? (Recycle the cans. Cans are made out of metal that comes from the ground. If we recycle them, we won't use up all the metal.) What do you recycle at home?
• To whom does the earth belong?
• How can we take care of it?
• How did the people in our story take care of the earth?

Landscape

Ingredients
fresh broccoli spears
celery stalks
carrot sticks
soft cream cheese
vegetable dip

Kitchen Tools
small paper plates
plastic spoons
paper towels

Guide Each Child To
1. Spoon cream cheese onto his plate and spread into a little hill on part of the plate.
2. Spoon vegetable dip onto another part of the plate.
3. Stand broccoli spears and celery stalks in the cream cheese hill.
4. Set carrot stick "logs" around to make a landscape.
5. Eat his landscape.

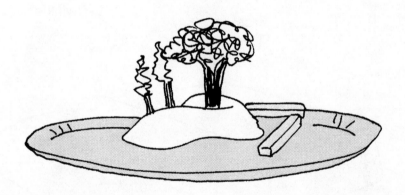

Suggested Bible Stories
Adam's Job
Bitter Water Turns Sweet
David Sings
Jesus Feeds 4,000 (Jesus' friends picked up leftovers)

Talk About
• What do we use trees for?
• Why is it good to plant trees?
• Who made the earth?
• How can we take care of it?
• How did the people in our story take care of the earth?

Cake Bed

Ingredients
ready-made pound cake
Twinkie
ready-to-spread frosting

Kitchen Tools
baking sheet or cake platter
plastic knife
paper plates
paper towels

Prepare Ahead of Time
Cut the top of the pound cake so that it's flat all the way across. Place it upside down on a baking sheet or cake platter to make a bed.

Guide Each Child To
1. Help place a Twinkie across one end of the pound cake for a pillow.
2. Help frost the bed with ready-made frosting.

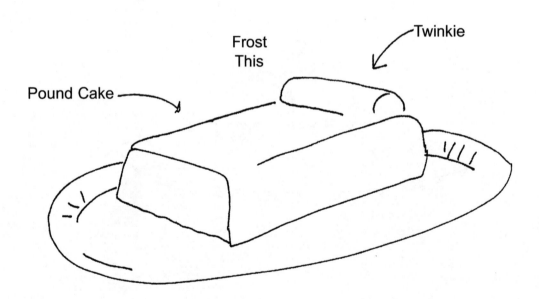

Frost
This

Twinkie

Pound Cake

Suggested Bible Stories
Joseph at Potiphar's House
Taking Care of the Worship House
Good, Wise People
The Lost Coin

Talk About
• How do people keep beds clean and neat?
• How do you take care of your room? Why?
• How did the people in the story take care of their places?

Friendship Punch

Ingredients
carbonated lemon-lime drink
two maraschino cherries per child
fruit juice (any flavor)
two slices of lime per child

Kitchen Tools
small paper cups
paper towels

Guide Each Child To
1. Choose a partner.
2. Let the teacher give one partner a cup of carbonated lemon-lime drink and two maraschino cherries.
3. Let the teacher give the other partner a cup of fruit juice and two slices of lime.
4. Take two empty cups and share by putting half of his drink in the empty cup and giving the other half to his partner.
5. Let his partner share his cherries and lime slices to add to his punch.

Suggested Bible Stories
Abraham and the Three Visitors
Rahab and the Spies
Ruth
David and Jonathan
A Widow Shares With Elijah
Elisha's Room on the Roof
Through the Roof
The Good Samaritan
Jesus and the Children
Jesus Washes His Friends' Feet
Paul in a Basket
Dorcas
Lydia
Paul and Silas in Prison

Talk About
• How are you being kind to each other?
• What are some other ways to be kind?
• How were the people in our story kind to each other?

Hot Cider

Ingredients
1 quart apple juice
1 quart cranberry juice
2 Tablespoons lemon juice
1 cinnamon stick
3 cloves
1/4 teaspoon allspice
1/4 teaspoon nutmeg

* If you don't have access to a stove, use a microwave or hot plate to heat the cider.

Kitchen Tools
stove*
large pan
long-handled spoon
ladle
Styrofoam cups
paper towels

Caution
Carefully supervise the children when drinking hot cider.

Guide Each Child To
1. Help mix together the cider.
2. Wait quietly as the teacher warms the cider. (It's best not to get it steaming hot for young children.)
3. Sip the cider after the teacher fills her cup and says it's cool enough for her to drink.

Suggested Bible Stories
Burning Bush
David, the Shepherd Boy
David and Goliath
Paul on Malta

Talk About
• In winter, hot drinks often taste good to us. That's because in many places, winter is cold.
• What would you see outside in winter? What would you hear?
• Is God with you in the winter?
• Is there ever a time God leaves you?
• How did God show the people in our story that He was with them?

Peanut Butter Sesame Balls

Ingredients
3/4 cup peanut butter
1/2 cup honey
1 teaspoon vanilla
toasted sesame seeds
3/4 cup skim milk powder

Kitchen Tools
large bowl
spoon
refrigerator
tray or platter
paper towels

Guide Each Child To
1. Help mix together peanut butter, honey and vanilla in the large bowl.
2. Add 1/4 cup of toasted sesame seeds and mix together.
3. Add skim milk powder and mix with the spoon, then mix with her hands.
4. Help shape the mixture into balls and roll in toasted sesame seeds. Chill in refrigerator.

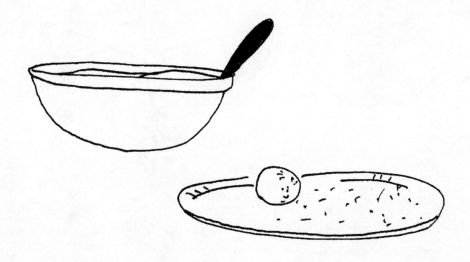

Suggested Bible Stories
Hannah Prays for a Baby
Daniel and the Lions (Daniel prays)
Jesus in Gethsemane
The Lord's Prayer
A Pharisee and a Tax Collector Pray

Talk About
• We are so glad God gives us good things to eat! How can we thank Him?
• Does God hear us?
• When can we pray? Where can we pray?
• What else can we pray about?
• Who prayed in our story? What happened?

Moon Apples

Ingredients
apples

Kitchen Tools
knife for teacher
paper towels

Guide Each Child To
1. Watch the teacher as she peels and slices the apples into wedges.
2. Take some apple "moons" to eat.

Suggested Bible Stories
Creation of Sun, Moon, and Stars
Jacob's Dream
Joseph's Dreams
The Sun Stands Still
Gideon
Nicodemus Visits Jesus at Night

Talk About
• These apple slices look like a moon. When do you see the moon? Did you ever see the moon in the daytime?
• What other lights are in the sky?
• Does the moon always look like this? What shapes can it be?
• Who made the moon?
• It was nighttime in our story. What happened that night?

Picnic

Ingredients
cheese squares
crackers
juice boxes

Kitchen Tools
sheet or tablecloth
paper plates
paper towels

Prepare Ahead of Time
Slice the cheese into squares.

Guide Each Child To
1. Help spread the sheet on the floor.
2. Have a pretend picnic by sitting on the floor with her snacks.

Variation: Have an animal picnic by using animal crackers and peanut butter.

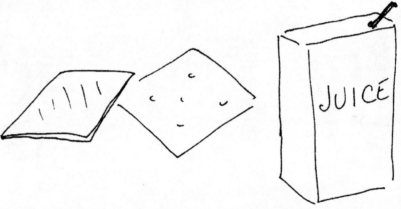

Suggested Bible Stories
Land:
Creation of Sky, Sea and Land
Garden of Eden
Abraham and Lot
Israelites Wander in the Wilderness
Twelve Spies
Animals:
Creation of Animals
Adam Names the Animals
Noah
Rebekah Gives Water to the Camels
Rachel's Sheep
Balaam's Talking Donkey
Saul Looks for Lost Donkeys
Solomon Knows About Animals
Ravens Feed Elijah
Daniel and the Lions
The Lost Sheep

Talk About
Land:
• Have you ever been on a picnic? Where did you go?
• What did you do at your picnic?
• Did you sit on the ground at your picnic? Who made the ground? Rocks? Sand?
• Tell about the land in our story. What was it like?
Animals:
• What kind of animal cracker do you have?
• What sound does that animal make? How does it move around?
• Who made animals?
• Which kind of animal is your favorite?
• Tell about the animal(s) in our story.

Food Textures

Ingredients
yogurt
vanilla wafers
a whole fresh pineapple

Kitchen Tools
plastic spoons
paper towels
paper plates
knife for teacher

Guide Each Child To
1. Put some yogurt and a vanilla wafer on his plate.
2. Take turns feeling the parts of the pineapple.
3. Watch as the teacher cuts the pineapple into bite-size pieces.
4. Taste the pineapple.

Suggested Bible Stories
Manna and Quail
Abigail Packs Food
Ravens Feed Elijah
John the Baptist
Jesus Makes Breakfast for His Friends
Jesus Feeds 5,000

Talk About
• Do all these foods look the same? Do they feel the same? Do they taste the same?
• How are they different? (Some are crunchy, some are smooth)
• Which do you like best?
• Who made these different foods?
• Who had food in the story? What happened?

Colorful Foods

Ingredients
dry donut-shaped cereal of different colors
fresh fruits and vegetables of different colors, such as:
• mandarin orange slices   • apples
• grapes cut in half   • bananas
• raisins   • carrot sticks

Kitchen Tools
paper plates
paper towels
knife for teacher

Prepare Ahead of Time
Wash, peel and cut the fruits and vegetables.

Guide Each Child To
1. Put some of the different colors and types of food on his plate.
2. Notice and identify the different colors of each food.

Suggested Bible Stories
Creation of Light and Color
Noah
Joseph's Colorful Coat
Birds and Flowers (Sermon on the Mount)
John Sees Heaven

Talk About
• Name some of the different colors of foods on your plate.
• Who made colors?
• Tell about the colors in our story.

Angel Crackers

Ingredients
rectangular and triangular-shaped crackers
peanut butter or cream cheese

Kitchen Tools
plastic spoon
paper plates
paper towels

Guide Each Child To
1. Put a generous dab of peanut butter or cream cheese on his rectangular-shaped cracker, about one-third of the way up. (Demonstrate this process for the children by making one for yourself and showing where everything goes.)
2. Take one triangular-shaped cracker and place one point on top of the dab of peanut butter or cream cheese.
3. Take another triangular-shaped cracker and place the point on top of the dab of peanut butter or cream cheese facing the other way (a mirror image of the first cracker). The triangles make the angel's wings.

Suggested Bible Stories
Adam and Eve Leave the Garden
Jacob's Dream
Balaam's Talking Donkey
Samson (angel tells of his birth)
Daniel and the Lions
Gabriel Appears to Mary
John the Baptist is Born
Angels Appear to the Shepherds
Joseph, Mary and Jesus Move to Egypt
The Resurrection (angels at the empty tomb)
Jesus Goes Back to Heaven
Peter Escapes From Prison

Talk About
• Who saw an angel in our story?
• What did the angel say?
• Who sent the angel? Why?

Hay Snacks

Ingredients
small squares of shredded wheat cereal
juice

Kitchen Tools
small bowls
paper cups
paper towels

Guide Each Child To
1. Place some shredded wheat squares in his bowl.
2. Help pour some juice into his cup.
3. Notice that the cereal looks like hay.

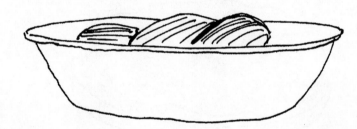

Suggested Bible Stories
Creation of Plants
Creation of Animals
Isaac Gets a Wife
Israelites Work for Pharaoh (straw made
   into bricks)
Jesus Is Born

Talk About
• This cereal looks like hay. What is hay?
• What kinds of animals eat hay?
• Tell about the animals (or hay, or straw) in
  our story.

Sheep Muffins

Ingredients
English muffins
soft cream cheese
raisins
spoon

Kitchen Tools
paper plates
paper towels
plastic knife or

Prepare Ahead of Time
Slice English muffins in half.

Guide Each Child To
1. Place one half an English muffin on her plate.
2. Spread cream cheese over the muffin.
3. Place two raisins on it for eyes, and one for a nose.

Suggested Bible Stories
Creation of Animals
Adam Names the Animals
Noah (animals)
David, the Shepherd Boy
David Plays the Harp (Psalm 23)
Angels Appear to the Shepherds
The Lost Sheep

Talk About
• This is our sheep muffin. Where are the eyes? Where is the mouth?
• Have you ever seen a sheep? What did it look like?
• Tell about the sheep in our story. What happened?

Healthy Foods

Ingredients

a variety of healthy snacks (choose as many as you want)
- apple slices
- pear slices
- peaches
- yogurt
- cucumber slices
- carrot sticks
- mandarin oranges
- blueberries
- raisins

Kitchen Tools

paper towels
paper plates
spoons for yogurt

Prepare Ahead of Time

Wash, peel and cut fruits and vegetables into bite size pieces.

Guide Each Child To

1. Choose two or three foods to put on his paper plate.
2. Eat his healthy snack.

Suggested Bible Stories

Naaman
Through the Roof
The Lame Man at the Pool
The Centurion's Sick Servant
Woman Touches Jesus' Hem
Ten Lepers
Jesus Heals the Bent Woman
The Man's Withered Hand
Peter and John Heal a Lame Man

Talk About
- Who gave us healthy foods to eat?
- Which food did you choose to eat?
- What is your favorite healthy snack?
- Why is it important to eat healthy snacks? (to keep us well)
- Who was sick in our story? What happened?

Cheese and Fruit

Ingredients

apple slices or bananas
three different types of cheese, such as:
• cheddar   • Swiss or Parmesan cheese
• a smoky-smelling cheese like Provolone

Kitchen Tools

paper plates, towels
knife for teacher

Guide Each Child To

1. Watch as the teacher slices the cheese.
2. Smell each cheese as the teacher puts them on her plate.
3. Watch as the teacher slices the apple.
4. Smell the apple slice.

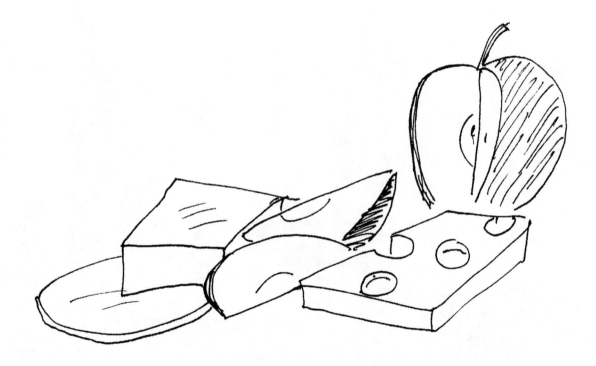

Suggested Bible Stories

Creation of Plants
Garden of Eden
Birds and Flowers
Perfume On Jesus' Feet

Talk About

• Did you like the different smells? Which was your favorite?
• What other things do you like to smell? Who made smells?
• How are we able to smell?
• Who made our noses?

Crackly Snack

Ingredients
puffed crispy rice cereal
milk

Kitchen Tools
small bowls
plastic spoons
paper towels

Guide Each Child To
1. Help pour a small amount of cereal in his bowl.
2. Help pour a small amount of milk in his bowl.
3. Listen for the crackly sounds.
4. Eat his snack and listen to the crunchy sounds.

Suggested Bible Stories
Birthright and Blessing
Samuel Hears God
David Listens for the Sound of Marching
The King Burns the Scroll
Jesus as a Boy in the Temple
The Wise Man's House
Mary and Martha
Blind Bartimaeus
Peter and Cornelius
Paul's Nephew Hears a Plot

Talk About
• What are some other foods that are noisy?
• What are some foods that are quiet?
• What's your favorite food?
• Who made our ears?
• Who does God want us to listen to?
• Who listened (or didn't listen) in our story? What did he or she hear?

Pizza Eyes

Ingredients
English muffins, one-half for each child
string cheese
jar of pizza sauce

Kitchen Tools
paper plates
paper towels
knife for teacher

Prepare Ahead of Time
Slice the string cheese into ?" slices. Cut enough so each child has two slices of cheese.

Guide Each Child To
1. Help pass out the paper plates, paper towels and plastic spoons.
2. Pray and thank God for his eyes and for the snack.
3. Put a small spoonful of pizza sauce on top of his muffin.
4. Let his teacher help by spreading the sauce around with the spoon.
5. Make pizza faces by putting two circles of cheese on the muffin to look like eyes.
6. Put a half a length of string cheese on the muffin to make a mouth.

Suggested Bible Stories
Birthright and Blessing
Blind Bartimaeus
Paul to Damascus

Talk About
• What color are the eyes on your pizza face?
• What color are your eyes?
• Who made your eyes?
• What was wrong with the eyes of the person in our story? What happened?

Star Sandwich

Ingredients
2 slices of bread for each child
peanut butter*
jelly

* If any child is allergic to peanuts, you may use
  cream cheese or pimento cheese.

Kitchen Tools
star-shaped cookie cutter(s)
paper plates
plastic knifes and spoons
paper towels

Guide Each Child To
1. Put two slices of bread on her paper plate.
2. Use the star-shaped cookie cutter to cut out a star from the middle of her bread slices.
3. Place a spoonful of peanut butter on one star.
4. Spread the peanut butter across the star.
5. Put a spoonful of jelly on the other star and spread it.
6. Put the two stars together and eat it.

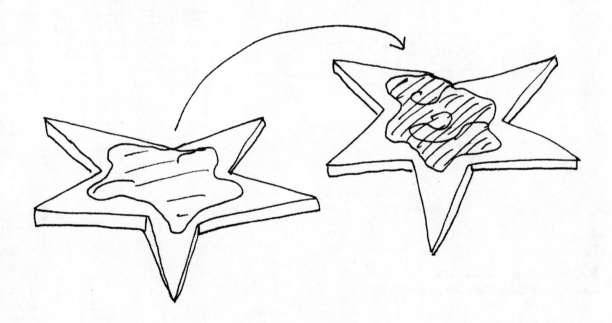

Suggested Bible Stories
Creation of Sun, Moon and Stars
God's Promise to Abraham
Jesus Is Born (the star over Bethlehem)
The Wise Men

Talk About
• What shape did we make?
• Where do we see stars? When do we see
  stars?
• What else is in the night sky?
• Tell about the star(s) in our story. What
  happened?

Water to Drink

Ingredients
fish-shaped crackers
water

Kitchen Tools
paper bowls and cups
paper towels

Guide Each Child To
1. Put some fish-shaped crackers in his bowl.
2. Help pour some water into his cup.

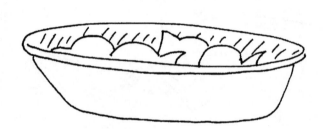

Suggested Bible Stories
Creation of Sky, Sea, and Land
Noah
Crossing the Red Sea
Water From a Rock
Crossing the Jordan
Jonah
Water Into Wine
The Great Catch of Fish
Jesus Stills the Storm
Jesus Walks on Water
Paul's Shipwreck

Talk About
• Where can we see water? (rivers, lakes, seas, ponds, waterfalls, rain, sinks, tubs, etc.)
• Who made the water?
• Tell about the water (rain, lake, etc.) in our story. What happened?

Buddy Mix

Ingredients
sugar
cinnamon
Chex cereal (any flavor)
raisins
vegetable oil

Kitchen Tools
measuring cups and spoons
paper cups
plastic spoons
paper towels
large zipper-locking plastic bag

Guide Each Child To
1. Help measure and mix 1 Tablespoon of sugar and 1/2 teaspoon cinnamon in a paper cup.
2. Pour 3 cups of cereal and 1 cup of raisins into the plastic bag.
3. Pour 1 Tablespoon of vegetable oil into the cereal/raisin mixture.
4. Close the bag and take turns shaking it so the mixture gets coated with oil.
5. Help pour the sugar/cinnamon mixture onto the raisin/cereal mix.
6. Close the bag and take turns shaking it again.

Suggested Bible Stories
David Thanks God
Singers Lead Jehoshaphat's Army
Daniel Thanks God
Ten Lepers

Talk About
• How are you helping to make our snack mix?
• Who is helping you?
• What should we tell people who help us?
• Who said thank-you in our story? Why?

Plant and Bird Snack

Ingredients
carrot sticks
apple slices
boiled eggs

Kitchen Tools
knife for teacher
paper plates
paper towels

Prepare Ahead of Time
Boil and peel the eggs. Wash and slice apples. Wash and slice the carrots into sticks. Leave one or two of each food whole so the children can see what it looks like before it's sliced.

Guide Each Child To
1. Put some carrot sticks and apple slices on her plate.
2. Guess what plant the carrot and apple comes from.
3. Look at the boiled eggs and guess what bird it comes from.
4. Watch as the teacher slices the boiled eggs.
5. Eat boiled egg slices, carrot sticks and apple slices.

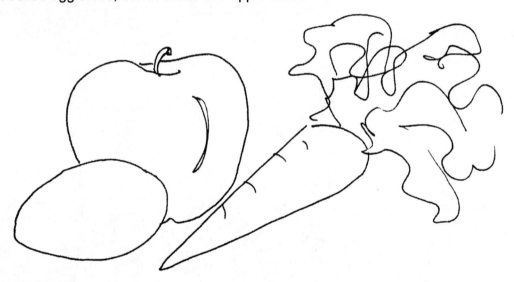

Suggested Bible Stories
Creation of Plants
Creation of Animals
Garden of Eden
Noah (sends out raven and dove)
Aaron's Staff Blooms
Ravens Feed Elijah
Jesus Is Baptized
Birds and Flowers (Sermon on the Mount)
Jesus in Gethsemane
The Resurrection (garden tomb)

Talk About
• Who made flowers and plants? Who made birds?
• What kind of plants do you like?
• What kind of birds do you like?
• Tell about the plants (or birds) in our story. What happened?

Cloud Crackers

Ingredients
graham crackers
non-dairy whipped topping

Kitchen Tools
plastic spoons
paper plates
paper towels

Guide Each Child To
1. Place a graham cracker on his paper plate.
2. Spoon a big scoop of whipped topping onto his graham cracker.

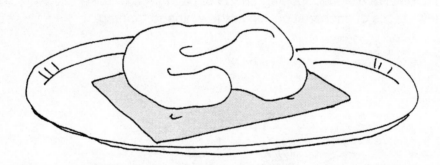

Suggested Bible Stories
Creation of Sky, Sea and Land
Elijah on Mt. Carmel (servant sees a cloud)
The Cloud Covers the Tabernacle
Jesus Goes Back to Heaven
John Sees Heaven

Talk About
• Does this snack remind you of something in our story? What?
• Are all clouds the same shape? The same size?
• Who made clouds?
• What happened with the cloud in our story?

95

Fruit Shortcake

Ingredients
ready-made sheet cake or pound cake
non-dairy whipped topping
bananas
can of mandarin oranges
blueberries

Kitchen Tools
knife for teacher
paper plates
plastic spoons and knives
paper towels

Prepare Ahead of Time
Open the can of mandarin oranges and drain the juice. If blueberries need to be washed, prepare the blueberries and store both fruits in a container until class time.

Guide Each Child To (Assign each child to do one or more of the following jobs to help.)
1. Help by passing out plates to everyone.
2. Help the teacher slice bananas.
3. Help place a slice of cake on each plate.
4. Help put a spoonful of whipped topping on top of each slice of cake.
5. Help put a few pieces of each fruit on top of the whipped topping.

Suggested Bible Stories
Abraham and the Three Visitors
Ruth
David and Jonathan
David and Mephibosheth
Elisha's Room on the Roof
Jesus Feeds 5,000
Jesus Makes Breakfast for His Friends
Lydia

Talk About
• How are we being kind, helping, and sharing with each other?
• How else can you be kind in class?
• How can you be kind at home?
• Why is it important to be kind?
• Who was kind in our story?

Raindrop Cookies

Ingredients
plain sugar cookies or vanilla wafers
white ready-made frosting
blue sugar cake-decorating sprinkles

Kitchen Tools
paper plates
plastic spoons and knives
paper towels

Guide Each Child To
1. Put a small scoop of frosting on her plate.
2. Use a plastic knife to frost her cookie.
3. Let the teacher place some blue sprinkles on her spoon.
4. Pretend the sprinkles is rain and sprinkle the "rain" on the white frosting to make raindrop cookies.

Suggested Bible Stories
Noah
The Plagues in Egypt
Elijah on Mt. Carmel
Jonah
Jesus Stills the Storm
Jesus Walks on Water
The Wise Man's House
Paul's Shipwreck

Talk About
• Who makes rain?
• What kinds of animals like rain?
• What do you like about rain?
• What is a storm like?
• Who saw the storm in our story? How did God take care of them?

97

Coin Chocolates

Ingredients
foil-wrapped, coin-shaped chocolate candies
juice

Kitchen Tools
paper towels
paper cups

Guide Each Child To
1. Help pass out the coin-shaped candy, two for each child.
2. Take one of his coins and give it to a friend in class. The friend gives him one of his coins. (Even though each child will give away one coin, he will get another coin in return and still have two coins.)
3. Help pour juice into his cup.

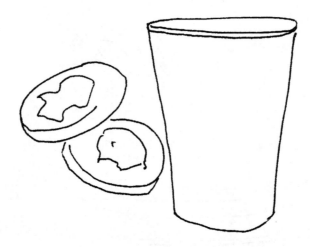

Suggested Bible Stories
Joseph's Brothers Move to Egypt
Hidden Treasure
The Pearl of Great Price
The Lost Coin
The Widow's Mite
Tax Money in a Fish

Talk About
• What does this candy look like?
• Do you have any coins at home? What kind?
• How did you get your money?
• Have you ever bought anything with your money?
• Who do we thank for our money? Why?
• How does God want us to use our money?
• Who used money in our story? What happened?

Baby's Cookies

Ingredients
baby cookies*
baby juice*

Kitchen Tools
paper cups
paper towels

* Try to get the type of infant cookies and juice
  which have a picture of a baby on the label.

Guide Each Child To
1. Look at the babies on the labels of the cookies and juice (if they have pictures of babies on them).
2. Help serve the baby cookies and baby juice.

Suggested Bible Stories
Isaac Is Born
Baby Moses
Hannah Prays for a Baby
Jesus Is Born

Talk About
• The cookies and juice you are eating are for babies.
• Do you have a baby in your house? Do you know someone who has a baby?
• What do babies do? What do babies need? How can we help take care of babies?
• Who gives us babies?
• Who was the baby in our story? What happened?

Our Restaurant

Ingredients

bread
peanut butter
jelly
cream cheese

pimento cheese
two kinds of juice
animal crackers

Kitchen Tools

paper plates
napkins
paper cups
paper towels

Prepare Ahead of Time

Make peanut butter and jelly sandwiches, cream cheese sandwiches, and pimento cheese sandwiches. Cut sandwiches in half.

Guide The Children To (Assign each child to do one or more of the following jobs to help.)

1. Pretend they are in a restaurant. Choose a few to be waiters, one child to be a cook, and the rest of the children to sit at the table.
2. Let the waiters ask each child, one at a time, what kind of sandwich they want. The waiters will then go tell the cook.
3. The cook places the chosen sandwich on a paper plate, and the waiter serves the "customers."
4. When all have been served, the waiters and cook may serve themselves and be seated.
5. Let the teacher choose a few children to take drink orders.
6. Allow the teacher to help pour juice for them and serve the customers.
7. After everyone is served, they may serve themselves and be seated.
8. Choose another child or two to serve animal crackers for dessert.

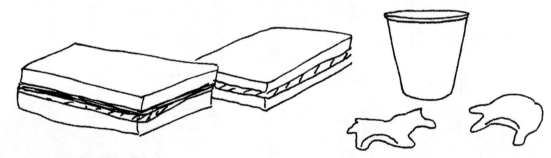

Suggested Bible Stories

Joseph In Potiphar's House
Israelites Work for Pharaoh
Building the Tabernacle
Rahab and the Spies
Deborah
David, the Shepherd Boy
Jesus Chooses Twelve Friends (the fishermen)
The Sower and the Seeds (the farmer)
Zacchaeus
Peter and Cornelius

Talk About

• What's your favorite restaurant? What workers does a restaurant need?
• What other kinds of workers live and work in our town? (Firefighters, police officers, mail carriers, etc.)
• Who gives us people to help us in our town?
• How can we respect them? (You may need to discuss what "respect" means.)
• What job did the person(s) in our story have?

Dipping Apples

Ingredients
apple slices
caramel or other dipping sauce for fruit

Kitchen Tools
paper plates
plastic spoons
paper towels

Prepare Ahead of Time (just before class)
Slice the apples.

Guide Each Child To
1. Choose a partner.
2. Let the teacher give partner A two apple slices and a spoonful of dipping sauce on her paper plate.
3. Let the teacher give partner B dipping sauce only.
4. Let the teacher ask partner A to give one of her slices of apple to partner B.
5. Eat the apple slices.
6. Let the teacher give partner B two apple slices.
7. Let the teacher to ask partner B to give one of the slices to partner A.

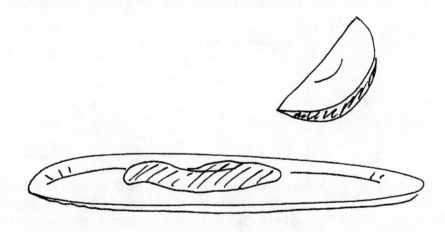

Suggested Bible Stories
Adam and Eve Eat the Fruit
The Ten Commandments
Naaman
King Josiah Finds God's Word
Recab's Family
Jonah
Jesus Is Tempted
The Wise Man's House
Two Sons and a Vineyard

Talk About
• You obeyed when I asked you to share. Sharing is the right thing to do.
• Who does God want us to obey? Why?
• Who obeyed (or disobeyed) in our story? What happened?

Choices

Ingredients
navel oranges
one square of unsweetened baking chocolate
one plain milk chocolate candy bar
1/4 cup salt
1/4 cup sugar

Kitchen Tools
paper plates
paper towels
knife for teacher
two small bowls for the
   salt and sugar

Prepare Ahead of Time Peel and section the orange.

Guide The Children To
1. Put a couple of orange slices on their paper plates.
2. Look at the bowls of salt and sugar and compare. Guess which is which without tasting them.
3. Dip an orange slice into the bowl of their choice and taste it to see whether it was salt or sugar. Eat their orange slices.
4. Look and compare the two pieces of chocolate. Decide which one looks like it will taste the best.
5. Let the teacher break off or cut a small piece of the one most children thought would taste best. Taste the chocolate they chose and then try the other piece of chocolate.

Suggested Bible Stories
Adam and Eve Eat the Fruit
The Ten Commandments
King Josiah Finds God's Word
Recab's Family
Jonah
Jesus Is Tempted
The Wise Man's House
Mary and Martha
Two Sons and a Vineyard

Talk About
- Was it hard or easy to tell the difference in the salt and sugar, and between the bitter and sweet chocolate, just by looking? Did you make the right choice and get the taste you wanted? Sometimes it's hard to choose what's right.
- If you are angry at someone, what would be a sinful or wrong choice to make?
- What would be a right choice?
- Does anyone in the world always make the right choice?
- What do we call wrong choices in the way we act and talk? (Sin)
- What do we call people who make wrong choices in the way they act and talk? (Sinners)
- How does God feel about sin? (Doesn't like it) How does God feel about sinners? (Still loves people who do wrong)
- Who made a choice in our story? Was it a good choice or bad choice?

Breaking Bread

Ingredients
dinner rolls
juice

Kitchen Tools
paper plates
paper cups
paper towels

Guide Each Child To
1. Help hand out the paper plates.
2. Let the teacher give every other child a dinner roll and keep one for herself.
3. Watch the teacher demonstrate as she tears the dinner roll in half and gives half of her roll to the child next to her.
4. Do the same thing the teacher did, giving half his roll to the child next to him.
5. Let the teacher give each child a roll who did not get to "break" the first roll.
6. Break his bread and give half to the child who shared his half previously.
7. Help pour juice. Eat his bread and drink the juice.

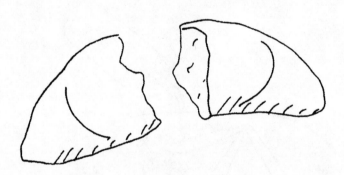

Suggested Bible Stories
Abraham and the Three Visitors
Joseph's Brothers Go to Egypt
Abigail Packs Food
A Widow Shares With Elijah
Jesus Feeds the 5,000
Mary and Martha
The Runaway Son
The Lord's Supper
Jesus Makes Breakfast for His Friends

Talk About
• Breaking bread is something people did in Bible times.
• Why do you think they called it that?
• Was it fun to tear the bread in half and share it with a friend?
• Friends like to eat together. Who do you like to eat with?
• Tell about the friends in our story who shared a meal.

Arrow Cheese Muffin

Ingredients
English muffins, one half for each child
canned processed cheese

Kitchen Tools
paper plates
paper towels
knife for teacher

Prepare Ahead of Time
Slice the English muffins in half.

Guide Each Child To
1. Place an English muffin on her plate.
2. Squirt canned processed cheese on top of her muffin in the shape of an arrow. (You will need to demonstrate how to do this.)

Suggested Bible Stories
Jericho's Walls Fall Down
Deborah
Gideon
David and Jonathan
Servant Sees God's Army
Singers Lead Jehoshaphat's Army

Talk About
• People used to fight with bows and arrows. Who was fighting in our story? Who won?
• How did God take care of the people in our story?
• How does God take care of you?

Kiss Candies

Ingredients
chocolate kiss candies
juice

Kitchen Tools
paper cups
paper towels

Guide Each Child To
1. Help pass out one or two chocolate kiss candies to each child.
2. Help pour juice for each child.
3. Peel the foil off their candies and eat. (You may need to help them with this.)
4. Help collect the foil candy wrappers and place in trash.

Suggested Bible Stories
Adam and Eve Have a Family
Isaac Gets a Wife
Jacob's Family (Jacob and Rachel)
Ruth
Esther

Talk About
• Whom do you love? Who loves you?
• Who are some people you love in your family?
• Who are some friends you love?
• How can you show somebody you love them?
• Who were the people in our story who loved (and helped) each other?

Color Cookies

Ingredients
plain sugar cookies or vanilla wafers
white ready-made frosting
sugar cake-decorating sprinkles (several colors)

Kitchen Tools
paper plates
plastic spoons and knives
paper towels

Guide Each Child To
1. Put a small scoop of frosting on her plate.
2. Use a plastic knife to frost her cookie.
3. Choose her favorite color of sprinkles.
4. Let the teacher put some colored sprinkles on her spoon.
5. Spread the sprinkles over the top of her cookie.

Variation: Divide the frosting into separate containers and make several different colors of frosting using food coloring.

Suggested Bible Stories
Creation of Light and Color
Noah
Joseph's Colorful Coat
John Sees Heaven

Talk About
• What is your favorite color? Who made colors?
• What other things are the same color as the sprinkles on your cookie?
• What had lots of colors in our story? What happened?

Turtles

Ingredients
1 cup butterscotch chips
2 Tablespoons margarine
1 cup powdered sugar
2 Tablespoons milk
1 cup peanuts
pecan halves, five for each child
stick pretzels

Kitchen Tools
microwave and bowl
sifter
waxed paper
refrigerator (optional)

Caution
Carefully supervise children.
Mixture will be hot.

Guide Each Child To
1. Help measure and mix the butterscotch chips and margarine.
2. Let the teacher melt the mixture in the microwave about 4 minutes at 50% power.
3. Help stir the mixture then sift the powdered sugar and add it to the chips mixture alternately with the milk.
4. Help stir in peanuts.
5. Help pass out waxed paper (one sheet for each child) and pecan halves (five for each child).
6. Arrange the five pecan halves on waxed paper as shown.
7. Let the teacher drop a heaping teaspoon of the peanut candy mixture in the middle, so the pecan halves are sticking out like a turtle's head and feet.
8. Snap a stick pretzel in half and stick it in the end to make a tail.
9. Allow the turtle to cool before eating. Refrigerate for faster cooling.

Suggested Bible Stories
Rebekah Gives Water to the Camels
Rachel's Sheep
Balaam's Talking Donkey
The Lost Sheep

Talk About
• What kinds of animals make good pets?
• Tell about your pet (or your neighbor's or grandma's).
• How can you be kind to pets?
• How were the people in the story kind to animals?
• Why does God want us to be kind to pets?

Breakfast

Ingredients
oranges
eggs
bread, one slice for each child
butter or margarine
salt

Kitchen Tools
toaster
fruit juicer (manual-type)
paper plates, cups
plastic knife
sharp knife for teacher
paper towels, napkins

Prepare Ahead of Time
Boil eggs, enough for each child to have one. Bring enough oranges to make a small amount of juice for each child. (Optional: If you prefer not to squeeze the oranges into juice, you could cut the oranges into small slices and serve.)

Guide Each Child To (assign the children to help with different tasks)
1. Help squeeze orange juice from fresh oranges.
2. Help the teacher make toast and butter each slice.
3. Help peel the boiled eggs.
4. Help pass out paper plates, napkins and cups.
5. Help pass out the eggs, toast and juice to each child.
6. Say a blessing before eating breakfast.

Suggested Bible Stories
Abraham and the Three Visitors
Joseph's Brothers Go to Egypt
Abigail Packs Food
A Widow Shares With Elijah
The Lord's Supper
Jesus Makes Breakfast for His Friends
Jesus Feeds the 5,000
Mary and Martha
Zacchaeus

Talk About
• Sometimes friends eat together. What do you like to eat with your friends?
• What is your favorite thing to eat for breakfast?
• Who ate together in our story?

Oatmeal Dough Animal

Ingredients
flour
water
oats
raisins

Kitchen Tools
large bowl
mixing spoon
measuring cups
waxed paper
paper towels

Guide Each Child To
1. Help mix 1 part flour, 2 parts oats and 1 part water.
2. Put some dough on a piece of waxed paper.
3. Mold the dough into the animal shape of his choice. Use raisins to decorate her animal.

Note: This is a dough that children can eat as they play. Make sure their hands are clean before they begin this activity.

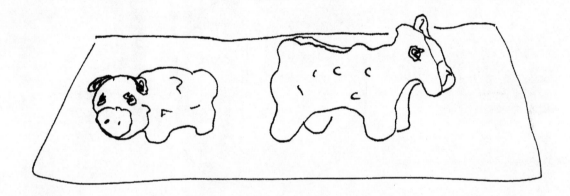

Suggested Bible Stories
Creation of Animals
Adam Names the Animals
Noah (animals)
Rebekah Gives Water to the Camels
Rachel's Sheep
Balaam's Talking Donkey
Saul Looks for Lost Donkeys
David, the Shepherd Boy
Daniel and the Lions
Ravens Feed Elijah
Jesus Is Born
The Triumphal Entry
The Lost Sheep

Talk About
• What kind of animal are you making?
• What is your favorite animal?
• Who made animals?
• What kind of animal was in our story?
What happened?

Poco Clay Handprint

Ingredients
peanut butter
powdered milk
honey
oats
coconut

Kitchen Tools
large bowl
mixing spoon
measuring cups
paper plates
paper towels

Guide Each Child To
1. Help mix equal parts of peanut butter and powdered milk.
2. Add honey until the mixture is thick.
3. Stir in oats and coconut.
4. If the clay is too sticky, add more powdered milk.
5. Flatten the dough on her paper plate.
6. Place her hand flat in the clay and make a hand print.

Note: This is a dough that children can eat as they play. Make sure their hands are clean before they begin this activity.

Suggested Bible Stories
Healing:
The Man's Withered Hand
Woman Touches Jesus' Hem
Blind Bartimaeus
The Lame Man at the Pool
Helping:
Rebekah Gives Water to the Camels
Baby Moses (Miriam helps)
Rahab and the Spies
David and Goliath
Friends:
David and Jonathan
The Fiery Furnace
Jesus Makes Breakfast for His Friends
Paul and Silas in Prison
Paul With Aquila and Priscilla

Talk About
Healing:
• Jesus healed a man's hand. How did Jesus heal him?
• Did you ever hurt your hand? What happened?
• How do we pray for people who are sick or hurt?
Helping:
• These are your helping hands. How can you help at home? How can you help in class?
• How did the person in our story help?
Friends:
• Sometimes friends shake hands. How else do friends act toward each other?
• What do you like to do with your friends?
• Who were the friends in our story? What happened?

Index

Index

Index

Index

Index

Index

Index

Index

Index

Index

Index